Greg brings a convicting message that beckons our attention in these times. If we are not diligent to press into greater measures of faith, we will be tempted toward complacency and half-hearted efforts. May these pages spark a fire that reminds us of the significance each day offers. *Never Settle* is a resounding call to embrace the wholehearted passion of the Christian life.

REBEKAH LYONS, bestselling author of *Rhythms of Renewal* and *You Are Free*

Greg Holder is a gifted teacher with a profound Christian faith who has much to offer all of us in need of godly help and encouragement.

NICKY GUMBEL, vicar at Holy Trinity Brompton; pioneer of the Alpha Course

There's more to your life than you can possibly imagine, and *Never Settle* will help you unlock the door to the more, more, more that God has for you. Prepare to be challenged, inspired, and encouraged with every page.

MARGARET FEINBERG, author of *More Power to You*

I have personally seen the results of Greg's leadership at The Crossing Church. As a guest speaker, I have experienced the hospitality of the staff, the vision of the church, and an organizational culture that never settles for less than their best for God. I'm excited you get to experience that now, too, through Greg's new book. My hope is that you are inspired to do the same. To rise up, dust yourself off (if life has knocked you down), and be reminded—never settle. God's with you. The two of you are a powerful combination.

JEFF HENDERSON, author of *Know What You're FOR*; pastor; entrepreneur

Greg infuses *Never Settle* with the same crackling energy, engaging humor, historical and geographical context, and spiritual truth that he presents in person. This book is alive, inviting and compelling us to fully engage and to fully live!

MIKE MANTEL, CEO of Living Water International

Never Settle is the best of both an all-out challenge to live differently as followers of Christ, and a beautiful reminder of who we are in Him. I could not echo this message more during this time: for people to know that their life matters and that they can live in the abundance of who He calls them to be, today.

SADIE ROB HUFF, speaker; *New York Times* bestselling author of *Live Original, Live Fearless,* and *Live*

Never Settle is a practical road map that will lead you out of a lukewarm, bland faith and into a vibrant Kingdom life. Greg calls us to a fresh experience with God—to actively seeking more with Him. With chapters on resilience, hospitality, and the impact of one life, Greg's encouraging message shines a spotlight on the miraculous things God is doing through ordinary people like us. This book is a perfect addition to any leader's toolbox because there has never been a more significant time in our culture to vow to never settle.

EDGAR SANDOVAL SR., president of World Vision U.S.

An equally challenging and inspiring book for followers of Jesus to step up. This is a powerful and provocative call to action for leaders in these days—and a needed reminder that we're made for something more.

BRAD LOMENICK, founder of BLINC; author of *H3 Leadership* and *The Catalyst Leader*

I love that *Never Settle* is a book about culture that isn't primarily about culture. It puts culture, loving people, and being a world changer into its proper perspective, which is enveloped within the holy Word of God. In such polarizing and confusing times, the church desperately needs to be reminded of the simplicity of this. I cannot "Amen" it any louder!

JOHN L. COOPER, singer; founder of Skillet

I have known Greg for many years. He lives what he writes. And what he's given us in *Never Settle* is a wake-up call to step into the life God created us for. To play our part in bringing the Kingdom of God to Earth in our everyday lives. And to never settle for anything less than God's vision for us, for his Church, and for this world!

JARRETT STEVENS, co-lead pastor of Soul City Church; author of *Praying Through* and *Four Small Words*

Choices,
Chain Reactions
& the Way Out of
Lukewarminess

NEVER SETTLE

GREG HOLDER

NavPress®

*A NavPress resource published in alliance
with Tyndale House Publishers*

NavPress is the publishing ministry of The Navigators, an international Christian organization and leader in personal spiritual development. NavPress is committed to helping people grow spiritually and enjoy lives of meaning and hope through personal and group resources that are biblically rooted, culturally relevant, and highly practical.

For more information, visit NavPress.com.

Never Settle: Choices, Chain Reactions, and the Way Out of Lukewarminess

Copyright © 2020 by Gregory Holder. All rights reserved.

A NavPress resource published in alliance with Tyndale House Publishers

NAVPRESS and the NavPress logo are registered trademarks of NavPress, The Navigators, Colorado Springs, CO. *TYNDALE* is a registered trademark of Tyndale House Ministries. Absence of ® in connection with marks of NavPress or other parties does not indicate an absence of registration of those marks.

The Team: Don Pape, Publisher; David Zimmerman, Acquisitions Editor; Elizabeth Schroll, Copy Editor; Eva M. Winters, Designer

Cover illustration of ice cube copyright © blueringmedia/iStockphoto. All rights reserved.

Cover illustration of flame copyright © Roi and Roi/Adobe Stock. All rights reserved.

Author photo by Tony Mellinger LLC, copyright © 2019. All rights reserved.

Published in association with the literary agency of Mark Sweeney and Associates.

Some of the anecdotal illustrations in this book are true to life and are included with the permission of the persons involved. All other illustrations are composites of real situations, and any resemblance to people living or dead is purely coincidental.

For information about special discounts for bulk purchases, please contact Tyndale House Publishers at csresponse@tyndale.com, or call 1-800-323-9400.

ISBN 978-1-63146-635-9

Printed in the United States of America

26	25	24	23	22	21	20
7	6	5	4	3	2	

For Brooks Holder, my father,
and Russ Kirkland, my friend.
Two heroes who never settled in their
pursuit of God's best for their lives.

CONTENTS

Foreword *ix*

Prologue: Choices, Chain Reactions & the Way Out *xi*

1 What Makes Jesus Puke *1*

2 Hobbits, Refugees & the *Imago Dei* *11*

3 Living in a VUCA World *25*

4 The Real Bat Cave *39*

5 Choose You This Day *57*

6 Chain Reaction *73*

7 Run to the Border *89*

8 Antifragile . . . Sort Of *105*

9 Zambezi Overload *121*

10 Muppets in the Balcony *137*

11 Welcome Aboard *155*

Epilogue: Music of the Dawn *177*

Acknowledgments *187*

Questions for Group Discussion *191*

Notes *199*

FOREWORD

IT WAS 12:00 A.M. in the lobby of a London hotel. A crowd of influencers were surrounding a leader whom I had been watching lead with passion throughout this trip. Different people had encouraged me to meet with him, claiming it was "necessary." I joined the crowd and yelled, "Greg! Is this our moment?"

Greg yelled back, "Sam! I think it is."

For the rest of the evening, his team and I wrestled with the complexities of doing ministry in an increasingly post-Christian society. Laughter continued, until his team eventually "threw up the deuces" (which means they left), going back to their rooms for a good night's rest.

It was now down to only three of us: two African American Christian leaders and Greg, a Caucasian pastor, in a hotel lobby in the heart of London. What would we possibly talk about?

For the next hour, Greg listened, asked questions, and ideated about racism in America and around our world. And then our discussions traveled from ministry and family life to poverty and economic empowerment, from Millennials and Gen Zers to prejudice and our hopes and dreams for the Kingdom. The one rule Greg gave us was to be as honest as possible.

After that night, I was convinced this man was determined to never settle for the status quo.

A question we should always ask when picking up a book is: *Has the author lived out the concepts and principles of the book he has written?* I can assure you Greg Holder has; I've seen it firsthand. I've also seen what a never-settling mindset can produce: greatness.

So, what about you? Do you believe that God is still up to something in our world? Do you want to leave a legacy? Do you want a life that is more than lukewarm?

If you answered yes to any of those questions, this book is for you. Whether it's the spark that starts a revolution or the missing puzzle piece you've been looking for, this book can inspire and challenge you to live a never-settled life, if you'll let it.

Greg Holder is the real deal. Will you trust him for a few hundred pages, knowing that his heart for you is just as big as his desire to see you unearth everything God has already placed in you?

(By the way, just in case you still care: This is a really good book!)

Sam Collier
International speaker and founder of A Greater Story Ministries

PROLOGUE

*Choices, Chain Reactions
& the Way Out*

OUR PLANET AND THIS EVER-INCREASING human herd are in
need of some serious—*and I mean supernatural*—help.

Anyone disagree?

Probably not.

Just catch a whiff of the latest scandal or injustice that leaves
us outraged, disillusioned, or just plain heartbroken. Listen, if
you can stand it, to the pundits shouting so loudly at each other
you can hear them two channels over. Everyone has an opinion
on what needs to change. Yet nothing seems to change. Watch
the splits widen and the rifts deepen between people who used
to at least tolerate each other. Feel creation itself tossing and
turning beneath our feet and—in the words of the apostle Paul
in Romans 8—"groaning" in pain. And that's before a global
pandemic.

So, the world is in need of some serious help.

It's discouraging.

Even intimidating.

What are we to do in the face of it all?

Oftentimes, we settle.

A LOADED WORD

The word *settle* has meant different things to people throughout the years. *Settling down* might be exactly what a young couple wants to do. Small children who are told to *settle down*, however, see it quite differently. To *settle our differences* is a good thing. When the *dust settles*, we're relieved. Most of us will settle debts and some might even settle bets. In the last few decades, the word *settle* picked up another meaning: to accept how things are, no matter how much you might want them to change. Now synonymous with "giving up," everyone from corporate leaders to coaches to innovators to personal trainers exhort us NOT to settle.

For many, it is a word now loaded with defeat.

It might not surprise you to learn that the earliest meanings of the word *settle* were related to the notion of resting. Eventually this led to the idea of making someplace your home. For better or worse, most people can conjure up an image of settlers doing what settlers do on some vast frontier: They stop going any farther. This will now be where they live for the rest of their days. They have *settled*.

We could riff on the history of this word for a few more fun-filled paragraphs, but let's stop here. Notice the connection between the newer meaning and the old one:

> *To settle* is the acceptance of the way things are—even when we long for better.
>
> *To settle* is also the decision to live in a place for the rest of your days.

When we settle, not only do we stop progressing, we also start putting down roots in a land of less than: less than satisfying, less than interesting, less than helpful, and certainly less than hopeful.

It's a choice we make—a costly one, at that.

A QUICK AND OBVIOUS DISCLOSURE

I wrote this book for anyone who—like me—has been tempted to settle for less than what God has for them. That means this is written from the perspective of someone who follows Jesus and values the Bible as a reliable source of wisdom, guidance, and truth. You may have noticed I've already referenced Scripture. It won't be the last time.

If you are one who struggles to understand such a faith (much less make it your own), you'll find what follows intriguing (I hope) and likely unfamiliar. To keep you in the conversation, I'll often give context to what we just encountered in Scripture before moving on to how it applies to our lives. Along the way, you may notice a rumbling hunger for more of this life and the promises mentioned. When this happens, pay attention. God is up to something, and you're being invited.

> To settle is the acceptance of the way things are—even when we long for better.

For those who already believe, as I do, that Jesus is the world's one true Lord come to set things right, you, too, are being invited to consider bold moves that just might seem as risky and counterintuitive and (ultimately) as life-giving as any you've made.

Or you can choose to settle.

Rarely do we consciously choose a "less than" life. And yet, it happens. Little by little, we give up. The world is, after all, in serious need of help.

What's the use of trying?

PLAYING IT SAFE

"It's too ugly *out there*," so the thinking goes. "I'll just hang out with people with whom I agree until Jesus returns." And with that, we retreat, raise the drawbridge, and relish our comfort. Meanwhile, the walls of our little fortresses (not to mention our hearts) grow thicker and thicker. In our isolation, we care less and less about anyone who isn't like us. We play it safe by retreating into comfortable circles of the like-minded.

Is it possible that the historic public health crisis of 2020 made this lurking fear grow even stronger? Followers of Jesus have always struggled with how to engage the world around us, and "social distancing" has only made the question murkier.

I wonder if this is why a recent Barna survey[1] shows that over half of US churchgoers have not even heard of the great commission. Just to refresh our minds: Jesus has been resurrected from the dead and will soon return to heaven, when he gives those first disciples (and the rest of his followers) their marching orders. At the end of the gospel of Matthew, we find these words: *Go and make disciples of all nations.*[2] This sounds an awful lot like going into the world, not retreating from it.

Were the challenges and dangers any less of an issue when Jesus first gave this charge? Hardly. Across the ages, those of us who have accepted God's grace through the work of his Son are to engage with those who might not look, sound, or believe like us. Aren't they, after all, the ones who need to see and hear the very Good News of how much they are loved by the God of all things?

Lest we fall into a common mistake, the great commission involves much more than dropping a couple nuggets of Scripture on our neighbors (though Scripture is certainly part of it). Jesus told us to be "teaching them to obey everything I have commanded you."[3] That's an awful lot for any who've forgotten his outrageous words of loving, serving, championing, forgiving, and yes, confronting in love.

To turn away from the world God loves in callous indifference is the exact opposite of what Jesus commanded. Lobbing the occasional judgment bomb over the castle walls is another mistake that counters everything Jesus taught.

Perhaps you've noticed how poorly this works.

Such a strategy holds no remedy for that which so disturbs us. Besides, it's terribly impractical for most people. Our daily existence requires we leave the castle every now and then. We still have to go to work or school on most days, or at least pick up the few things that can't be delivered to our homes by Amazon.

What, then, happens when we do go into the world?

BLENDING IN

The volume is already so loud in our world, we reason, the mention of anything objectively true is controversial. Taking a stand against an injustice is too radical. Making peace in a difficult situation is too risky. Such boldness might draw attention to us and our faith. More importantly, it might draw fire from those who disagree. Instead, we settle for blending into the crowd, the conversation, the community. We choose bland over bold.

> Following in the steps of Jesus will lead us to bold expressions of love, for which our world is aching.

Fear lies at the root of this decision. Our short-fused culture will explode at the slightest hint of anything that does not line up with the collective and ever-fluid definition of what is correct. Following in the steps of Jesus will lead us to bold expressions of love, for which our world is aching. Such a life will also fly in the face of this groupthink age.

Live as Jesus taught us and it's only a matter of time before the blowback blows our way.

This leads many to live a camouflaged Christianity. We settle for moving through the world as mere ghosts of our true selves. Present and noticed, but just barely.

PUTTING DOWN ROOTS

In making our home in the land of the bland, we begin settling in many ways.

We settle for:

. . . others doing the work.
. . . simple answers to complicated issues.
. . . shallow relationships.
. . . broad and bruising words.
. . . small and stunted dreams.

Of course, this list could go on and on, but I'm getting depressed and you're getting bored. How about one more that sums them all up?

We settle for so much less of Jesus.

Who he is and what he still wants to do for us, in us, and through us. That's it. Now we're getting somewhere.

SUPERNATURAL HELP

So, what's the use of trying in this world gone bad?

It might be a fool's errand except for the possibility of *supernatural help.*

Why wouldn't we expect such help?

"In the beginning God created the heavens and the earth."[4] The rest of the story rests on this truth. Ah, yes, this is a worldview, a way of perceiving reality (more on that in chapter 3) that informs everything. And from the beginning, this loving, powerful, artistic, completely-in-control God was in the midst of his creation, interacting with us creatures, who somehow bear his image (chapter 2).

We were made to do magnificent and noble things: to worship our Creator with full hearts, to love one another, and to care for this glorious gift of a home.

Of course, the choice to settle for so much less was first made in Genesis 3. From then on, our rebellion has stained every page of the story, and the effects are as obvious as they've ever been. Again, no breaking news here.

And yet, this is not the end of that story.

From the heartbreak of our first parents' first bad decision until the very moment you're reading this sentence, God has not given up on us or this world he once considered "very good."[5]

This is the foundation on which the rest of this book rests.

He is still at work in ways we can see and celebrate in our next breath (chapter 4). He is also at work in ways we cannot fully comprehend. Not yet. But oh, what our good and gracious God will reveal on that day which will never know the night. Injustice and evil, pain and loss will not have the final word.

Until then, we who live in the early morning—when dawn has only begun to push the darkness away—will live as children of the dawn (epilogue). We trust our King and take the next step. That's my way of letting you know the rest of these pages are not merely a lament of all that is going wrong and just how wrongly we are doing them. In fact, they will often be just the opposite: a reminder of what God is still doing in us, around us, and in spite of us—but often through us. At least what he *could yet do through us*.

Which brings us to the decision each of us makes daily, hourly, moment-by-moment: *Will we settle for less? Or will we choose God's glorious way?*

CHOICES CRACKLING WITH POWER

When I read my Bible, I discover more than a universe-wide plan to heal the battered and beautiful creation I see when I read my newsfeed. I find even more than the redemption of a stumbling human race, though God's plan is certainly all of this. Keep reading and the epic will include the personal. God speaks to Abraham of a nation, an entire world that will be blessed. But he also knows the old nomad by name and visits his home (chapter 11).[6]

Throughout the Scriptures, the vastness of the story always includes the very intimate. What God is still doing is both global and personal. This is the way out: It's both. I am the healed one. The redeemed one called to so much more than I first imagined. For his own good reasons, God is inviting me (and you) to be a part of the healing, the restoring, the making right of his world.

> Every choice in your day is crackling with God's redemptive power.

Clearly we will need supernatural help.

What follows, then, are not the great and rapturous triumphs of my life. They are merely truths I've noticed along the way—in Scripture (always), in the bumbling and accidentally interesting moments of my own life, and, mostly, what I have learned from the courage of others who keep teaching me what it means to never settle for less than the next step of obedience . . .

To Jesus. Always Jesus.

Here comes the help.

When he sends us into his broken but loved world in Matthew 28, Jesus also leaves us with a stunning promise: "I am with you always, to the very end of the age."[7] You want help? Jesus is supernaturally *with us*—his presence, his protection, his power—every step, every moment, every day until the very end.

That means every choice in your day is crackling with God's redemptive power.

Even the smallish moments of your life can start chain reactions of grace and goodness in unpredictable but far-reaching ways (chapter 6). Try to imagine what might yet happen in your next moment on this planet with the God who called everything into existence. He is the same God who calls you by name.

THE WAY OUT OF LUKEWARMINESS

To speak of a "way out" implies movement. Now is not the time to put down roots in the safe and predictable, for it is actually quite dull and deadening. The first step will be to break camp, pull up stakes, and, well, refuse to settle any longer.

What follows is, I hope, a way to re-engage the world God has not abandoned. There will soon be plenty of books devoted to the virus that crippled the world in early 2020. This book was written before talk of quarantines and social distancing. It does now seem, however, that a "way out" will also be a "way back in." The words of Jesus remain timeless, and his call to this different life predates this recent moment in history and will remain long after.

To jar us out of the assumption that we've heard it all before (we probably have) and tried it all before (we probably haven't), we will begin with some of the bluntest (and grossest) words Jesus ever uttered. Once we begin to understand what that famous quote truly means, we'll spend the rest of our time trekking out of the lukewarminess. Yes, I made that word up. But I hope you'll soon agree that it describes a certain kind of life we can no longer live.

Along the way, we'll encounter Spirit-infused ways of thinking and behaving in God's world. There is no formula to this life that refuses to settle, but there are a few mileposts to look for on this way out of a half-hearted existence.

At these everyday intersections, we will have more choices to make. Choices about how we view things (chapters 3 and 4), about how we react to conflict (chapter 7) and the challenges of life in a broken world (chapter 8). In chapter 9, the decision to wait on God wraps around a harrowing story. Chapter 10 is a twenty-first-century call to choose differently—and wisely—when it comes to our engagement with the digital world. To welcome another (chapter 11) with true hospitality might just be the timeliest of choices for these angry and fearful times.

Each step out of the tepid will set off chain reactions. Each decision can create ripples in our world for the glory of God. With each turn, the Spirit of God is waiting to transform you as he works through you. What happens next is not just for the world around you but for you. As C. S. Lewis reminds us:

> Every time you make a choice you are turning the central part of you, the part of you that chooses, into something a little different from what it was before.[8]

CHANGES AND CHAIN REACTIONS

The price of a book isn't inconsequential, unless someone gave this to you as a gift (If that's the case, the giver has exquisite taste). But the reading of a book—in a few sittings or over several months—will cost you. It will cost you time, which is valuable. It will cost you the effort of paying attention, which is difficult in these distracting times. It will also cost you the price of living a different life, for changes are not always easy.

So then why are you here, on this particular page of this specific book, in the middle of whatever your today holds? The reasons are many, no doubt. To now speak in lofty tones of how God led you to this page might seem a bit much—how could I possibly know what you need in this very moment? Absolutely true. What I know for sure is that the truth of God has elbowed its way into my thoughts and heart. I am only too familiar with the desperate longing for more than the ordinary.

I am increasingly aware that God is calling me to more. Perhaps you've sensed the same.

Consider this an invitation to a different way of thinking, of seeing the world, of living in the world.

But I must warn you: It will be a little unsettling.

Once we've settled into the safe and mediocre, pulling away from the status quo is inherently *unsettling*. But even this is a hint we are on the right track. Isn't that what we crave deep down—a different kind of thinking, loving, speaking, and doing that *makes a difference*? Such life doesn't always blend in. Instead, it jolts. It soothes. It heals. It endures. It restores. It leads. Above all, this life loves outrageously well, for without love, the rest amounts to nothing.[9]

This is a life aligned with the God of the universe.

This is a life tapped into the crackling energy of the one who made us for more and loves us more than we can imagine.

This is the way out of lukewarminess, and it will be worth it.

So listen up, buckle up, saddle up—whatever you need to do to get ready—and now, let's hurry up and turn the page . . . for God is still up to something, and the next moment starts now.

FOR PERSONAL REFLECTION

- Consider a time in your life when you settled for less. What choices lead you to that place? How did you feel in that moment?
- What do you hope to gain from reading *Never Settle*?

WHAT MAKES JESUS PUKE

WE WERE IN THE COLD, BLUE OCEAN off the southern coast of South Africa. Three families had piled onto a dive boat for one reason: to watch a few of us get up close and personal with some of the great white sharks that troll those waters. Mind you, myself and two buddies were in a shark cage. But still, the moment beneath the water when one of those beasts lunged and chomped at "my" corner of the cage is still fresh, years later.

That's why we ventured into those rolling seas that day. That's why we put on the wet suits and climbed into chilly water looking an awful lot like seals—which, as it turns out, is exactly what these sharks eat. But even that isn't enough to get their attention. Do you know the quickest way to bring sharks close to that cage? It isn't by tossing three tourists into the water. It isn't by bringing a cellist on board to play the theme from *Jaws*.

You appeal to their sense of smell. And what do they smell? Blood. Fish parts. Here's the technical term: you chum the water.

At this point, my two friends and I are still bobbing in the water (in the cage), waiting for some action to start beneath the surface. Sinking and swaying with every wave, enveloped in the exhaust of the boat engine and surrounded by the slimy slick of fish entrails. People ask, "Can you get seasick IN the water?"

Why yes, yes you can. Especially if one of those buddies—and here is where I'll stop with the detailed descriptions—decides to chum the waters as well.

But now the point (there's a point to this?): Whether it's at sea, in the air, or on dry land, most of us have been that kind of sick. There is something so disagreeable happening inside us that it leads to a moment we'd rather not think about.

Wow.

What an inspiring way to open the book. Why start things off this way? I am so glad you asked.

A SOBERING VISION

The book of Revelation has wild and powerful imagery that has sparked two thousand years of discussion about how to interpret this strange vision the apostle John experienced. Sometimes lost in all that is that John, the last living disciple, writes this letter to encourage specific churches in the last few years of the first century.

In chapter 1, John tells us he is in exile on a volcanic outcropping of an island called Patmos. It's Sunday, and he's overwhelmed by the Spirit of God—maybe he's praying or worshiping or just remembering all the things he saw with his own eyes all those years ago. Who knows? Memories of his days with Jesus, so rich and vivid, could still stir the heart of any worshiper. What we do know is that John hears a blaring voice that tells him to write down all that is about to happen and send it to seven specific churches in Asia Minor, what we would now call the country of Turkey.

Whose voice? Whose words? John makes this abundantly clear throughout. He turns around and sees a face he recognizes, but looks so very different: Jesus in all his glory. "His eyes were like blazing fire. . . . His voice was like the sound of rushing waters. . . . His face was like the sun shining in all its brilliance." The resurrected Lord of all said, "I was dead, and now look, I am alive forever and ever!"[1]

No wonder John collapsed at Jesus' feet.

Perhaps we, too, should be sobered, for these are the words of the resurrected King of the universe. And while they were meant for very specific situations in John's day, the sovereign Lord still speaks to churches and Christians throughout the ages.

THE FAMILIAR PUNCH LINE
THAT NEEDS EXPLAINING

This will not be a step-by-step account of John's fantastic vision. Alas, for some, this might be a disappointment. (Sorry.) For others, perhaps those fearing they might be left behind in an elaborate discussion involving charts and timelines, this comes as a relief. Instead, we will allow the shocking words Jesus directed toward one church—at Laodicea—to rattle our thoughts and stir our imaginations. These words will then serve as a backdrop for why the rest of this book even matters.

The punch line in this passage will be familiar to many, yet without context, the way it's sometimes explained hasn't been helpful.

> "I know your deeds, that you are neither cold nor hot. I wish you were either one or the other! So, because you are lukewarm—neither hot nor cold—I am about to spit you out of my mouth."[2]

These are the words of the one who speaks truth because he IS truth. These are the words of the ruler of God's creation. Never forget: These are the words of Jesus . . . and he doesn't sound all that pleased.

If Jesus is this upset (and we'll see just how upset in a moment), shouldn't we be bothered? If his words prove to be unsettling, shouldn't we be unnerved? And shouldn't we want a better understanding of what has upset him so?

THE EXPLANATION THAT MAKES NO SENSE

To fully appreciate what's being said, we need a little review of ancient geography. Laodicea. It was founded in the 200s BC and was situated in a river valley along with two neighboring cities. To the north, about six miles on the opposite side of the valley, sat Hierapolis. To the east a few miles upriver was the city of Colossae.

And in between, at an intersection of major trade routes, was Laodicea—well-known and well-off and, well, a city with a church that had lost its way.

Now that we have our bearings, it's time to understand exactly what Jesus is saying to these Christians. Is it, "I'd rather you be for me or against me—don't just sit on the fence?" I remember hearing it explained that way growing up; perhaps you did, as well. We are not alone. Eugene Peterson writes about this passage and the church leaders of his youth: "High on every pastor's agenda was keeping people 'on fire' for Jesus."[3] Here's how authors Richards and O'Brien summarize this explanation: "'Hot' (committed) was best, but 'cold' (lost) was preferable to 'lukewarm' (nominal) because it was honest!"[4] Is that the point here—to keep people's faith "red hot?" And if we can't do that, "stone-cold dead" is better, because at least it's honest?

That makes no sense.

When would Jesus ever want his followers to oppose him in cold indifference? Remember he is speaking to his church, so let's not make this something it's not.

FENCE-RIDING IS STILL TO BE AVOIDED

To be honest, there is a kernel of truth to the point some have stretched to make. If we just sit on the fence and refuse to commit to any action, if we wear a piece of religious jewelry around our neck but the value and meaning of the Cross never seeps into our heart, if we try faking our way through all of this Jesus business, I believe it does affect him greatly.

He's never interested in fence-riding.

God does not want shallow pleasantries and empty words tossed at him anymore than we do. So yes, the further into this discussion we go, the more you'll begin to realize that life with Jesus is ultimately an all-or-nothing proposition. The gospel invitation is intense and demanding—there is too much talk of crosses and dying to suggest otherwise. We cannot and should not avoid that reality.

> God does not want shallow pleasantries and empty words tossed at him any more than we do.

But this does not fully explain these strange words.

Fortunately, there are clues in our geography lesson that can help us understand what this punch line meant to those Laodiceans. From there, it becomes much easier to apply Jesus' words to our own lives.

THE EXPLANATION THAT MAKES SENSE

With a bit more background of the region, this passage comes into full view.

The city to the north, Hierapolis, sat atop 300-foot-tall, snow-white cliffs. In fact, today the town is called Pamukkale, or "cotton castle" in Turkish. The calcium deposits still billowing over that cliff are the result of hot springs bubbling out of that hill. You see, this was (and is) a town known for its hot springs.

Two thousand years ago, this was already a spa town.

And why not? When you are injured, sore, or just plain tired, there is something soothing—restorative, some would say—about the water of hot springs. From emperors to commoners, Hierapolis was a place to go for comfort and healing.

The city to the east, Colossae, lies near the foot of Mount Cadmus. Because of its location beside this snowcapped mountain, cold, refreshing spring water always flowed.

Two thousand years after Jesus' words, people bottle water like that and sell it at exorbitant prices.

When your throat's dry and your tongue sticks to the roof of your parched mouth, there is nothing that quenches that thirst like cold, clear water. Water that was abundant in little Colossae.

Now we're getting to the heart of Jesus' message.

To the north were famous hot springs. To the east, the cold, refreshing waters. What word best described Laodicea's water supply? (Go ahead, take a guess.) Lukewarm.

For all of this city's strengths, it had one major weakness: a lack of good water. As a result, water had to be brought in via the Roman aqueduct system. And yes, by the time it got there, the water was neither hot nor cold but lukewarm. What's worse, it was so full of minerals that the water wasn't just warm, it smelled and tasted funny and could actually make you a little sick when you drank it.

I told you we were getting there.

It's easy to see, in this context, how "hot" and "cold" are both good. The hot springs bring healing. The cold mountain streams quench thirst. But the lukewarm, stinky water of Laodicea isn't all that helpful. In fact, it was hard to stomach.

> [Jesus said,] "Because you are lukewarm—neither hot nor cold—I am about to spit you out of my mouth."

NOW THE GROSS PART

The word translated "spit" is the Greek word *emeo*, from which we get our word *emesis*. In case you're not connecting these dots, an emesis pan is that funny-shaped thing they give you in the hospital if you're going to be sick. An "anti-emetic" is medicine given to prevent you from getting so sick you need that little pan. This leads us to the meaning of that Greek verb: vomit. If you're not going to use a word like vomit or puke or hurl or . . . (that was the absolute limit I was given on this point), then try the old King James translation: "I will spue thee out of my mouth."

When we get truly nauseated, when something so disagreeable is happening that we can't stomach it any longer, it leads to a moment we'd rather not talk about.

Jesus has come to such a moment with this church.

Something so unsavory gurgles in the lives of these people that our Savior cannot stomach it any longer. Nor can we ignore it any longer in our own midst. The words of Jesus are clear, and they still apply: *I know your deeds.* The unrivaled and not-to-be-trifled-with God of glory says, "I can see what's happening, and it's got to stop."

THE UNSETTLING TRUTH

What is it that makes Jesus want to puke?

When those who call themselves Christian decide to play it safe and compromise. When people grow so satisfied with how they're doing in this world that it never occurs to them to bring relief to others. When those whose hearts have been healed, whose destinies have been forever altered, simply forget the spiritually (and physically) thirsty. When those of us who have been graced with new life refuse to engage a dying world desperate for answers.

If such an approach to life disturbs Jesus so much that it makes him sick, we must not look away in faux disgust at his language.

Perhaps it is time for us to be good and disgusted about the right things, to be offended by the mediocre and ineffective. Our Lord is calling us to so much more, and the invitation has never been more timely.

The marching orders of Matthew 28 are clear: Go and tell others the story of the God who loves people enough to make a way, the God who gave up his right to get even . . . tell them about the gift of grace and the promise of his presence. And do something outrageous along the way: Love others as you have been loved. Go into this hurting and desperate world with more than good words. Take action.

> Be hot or cold, but *do* something.

Let's be soothing and shocking as the situation calls for. Be hot or cold, but *do* something. By God's grace, the world will change again. But by his grace, so, too, shall we.

Anything less sickens our Savior.

A KNOCK ON THE DOOR

I am so thankful Jesus finishes this very tough talk with words of hope and restoration—*I'm giving you such a stern correction out of love . . . now repent, come back to me.* We'll come back to that word *repent* and this story in a few chapters, because it is just too good to leave alone. For now, notice the last image of Jesus in this passage isn't a shocking one. Well, it is shocking, in its humble and pursuing love.

> Here I am! I stand at the door and knock. If anyone hears my voice and opens the door, I will come in and eat with that person, and they with me.[5]

If we'd just open the door . . . he knows what we were made for. He knows where the story is heading. He knows what we long for and what we're capable of. He knows. He knows what our relationships can be like. He knows what it will be like for us to connect with what he is still doing in this world. He knows how the world will be blessed if we will but join him.

It will look slightly different at times, this following Jesus into the world. But look closer, for there are similarities.

When you teach a child to read. When you care for a spouse or parent suffering from dementia. When you forgive someone. When you stand against an injustice. When you laugh deeply with someone. When you weep openly with another. When you give with no strings attached. When you intentionally allow the spotlight to find a colleague instead of you. When you whisper words of encouragement. When you serve in small ways most would never notice. When you honor someone older or younger than you. When you build a bridge to someone of a different ethnicity or sexual orientation. When you dare to do any of these things or a thousand others motivated by the pursuing love of Jesus, you are anything but lukewarm. You are hot and cold, soothing and shocking. You are telling his story to a world he has not given up on.

> Motivated by the pursuing love of Jesus, you are anything but lukewarm.

This is the beginning of a different life.

And get this: *You were made for such things.*

FOR PERSONAL REFLECTION

- Take inventory of your heart. Do you feel like you are shockingly cold and soothingly hot? Or does life feel lukewarm these days?
- What's one thing from this chapter that gives you encouragement as you're on this journey?

HOBBITS, REFUGEES & THE *IMAGO DEI*

UNDER AN OVERPASS, just off a busy intersection in Beirut, there lives a Kurdish family. The small concrete rooms accessed by an impossibly narrow hallway are nothing like the home they left in Syria. They are refugees from the recent war and now find themselves scrambling, improvising their way through what is becoming the new normal of their lives.

We cram into a small, bunker-like room. The warmth of a mother's touch defies the cold flicker of florescent light. A rug on the concrete floor, a couple of plastic chairs, laughing children, a squirming infant on the lap of his loving father.

I am sitting in someone's home.

The full story of this unlikely haven is for another time, but the plot runs through a local church that simply wanted to help a family in crisis. Yes, this is only one family. *But it is one family.*

Through a translator, they begin to tell their story— a certain few, Christians they are called, were the only ones to respond to their very real needs. It was not a grand, institutional gesture. No global initiatives here. Just people loving people in crisis. Tangible help. Words, yes, I'm sure, but so much more than words. And the effects of those very real actions were still rippling through this home.

Perhaps what they had been told of these "Christians" was not all true, the father muses. Could it be that some truth about these nonbelievers had been hidden from him by others? Somewhere along the way, the mother attended a Bible study. She is learning and now praying—*to Jesus*. She speaks of astounding answers to her very specific prayers to this Jesus. She can't explain it all yet, neither can she deny what is happening before her eyes. Her husband is now studying and learning more of this Jesus mentioned in the Qur'an and worshiped in the New Testament. Together, this family navigates a path of faith that is not as clear-cut or predictable as some would like.

But something has happened—is still happening—in their midst.

I'm reminded of the once-blind man in John 9 who tired of a theological debate with the muckety-mucks over the cause of his blindness. Instead of getting lost in all he did not know, he returned to what he did know: He used to be blind but now he could see. Those up to their eyeballs in theological insights couldn't see the miracle in front of them: A man had been healed! God was up to something beyond their expectations and explanations. And yet, these pious men missed it.

I didn't want to make their mistake sitting in this concrete bunker of a home. A loving couple with incomplete answers and fuzzy theology only knew what they knew: Followers of Jesus had loved them well. Jesus answers prayers. Jesus can be trusted.

It's a place to start.

BIG PRAYERS, BIGGER GOD

And then, in an evening full of surprises, one more: as passionate Arabic filled the room, a request was translated to us. The words from that father are still burrowing their way into my stunted imagination. A request as humble as it was audacious: "Please pray for me. I would like to go back home and tell the Kurdish people about Jesus."

Again, I'm not sure at this point how much he knows about Jesus. But what he does know is as real as anything in his life. All because a few people acted out of their own faith in this Jesus.

Is this how things change in a corner of the world where nothing seems to change? Am I being naive? Are such prayers expecting too much?

From whom?

Certainly not God. Hopefully, we can all agree he is still up to the challenge.

Is it expecting too much of one man? Maybe. We should be patient and wise here. Let's humble ourselves to experts such as our World Vision hosts, who know an awful lot about how things work in such difficult spaces. They will know how best to help him.

But let's not douse his dream.

This is, after all, how things often change—one life at a time. One faithful act at a time. It is how things began to change for this man—when someone took a risk and offered help. Do such moments always lead to instant conversions? Probably not as often as we pastors might suggest. Still, darkness is pushed back. Truth is spoken. Grace is offered. A family is blessed.

> This is, after all, how things often change— one life at a time. One faithful act at a time.

And with that, the world is a little different.

THE START OF SOMETHING BEAUTIFUL

It started with one moment and a longing to make things better.

Peter preached at Pentecost, and the church exploded into existence. Martin Luther nailed some ideas onto a door, and look what happened. Harriet Beecher Stowe picked up her pen and awakened a nation to the evils of slavery. Ruby Bridges walked to school through a sea of hate, and hearts softened along the way.

And the world, in small and not-so-small ways, changed.

None of these people were alone, of course. Nor should we ever dream of great things in isolation. As I argued in my previous book,[1] we were designed to accomplish great things together.

But it often starts when just one person refuses to settle for the easy and comfortable.

Who am I to say it can't happen again when God has already done so much under an overpass, just off a busy intersection in Beirut? That night, we prayed—in the great name of Jesus—for this impressive man and the people he loves. We cried and laughed and thanked our gracious hosts. Then we slipped back into the dark and chaotic night of the city. I may never know how far the gospel of Jesus reached into this refugee's world, at least not this side of eternity.

But I find myself still praying for him. And for me. What might happen if I lived with that kind of expectancy? What if I paid better attention to that gnawing in my gut telling me to take another step out of lukewarminess?

THE OBVIOUS POINT I'VE BEEN AVOIDING

This book can in some ways be summed up in a phrase I almost hesitate to type: *You can make a difference in this world.*

Ugh. Blech. Yawn. Here we are, two chapters in, and you're ready to give this book to your Aunt Ethel, who has the world's largest collection of inspirational self-help literature. I completely understand—the last thing you need is a "you can be whatever you put your mind to" piece of quasi-spiritual claptrap.

I pray this book is nothing of the sort.

Everything that follows traces back to the grace of God, the sacrifice of Jesus, and the very real presence of the Holy Spirit in the lives of those who have accepted the offer of a new and utterly different life. Put your self-help fears aside, and let's face the truth.

There is a reason many have visceral reactions to talk of "making a difference." Beyond the epidemic levels of cynicism today, there is a legitimate wariness of starry-eyed optimists. Why? Because the so-called answers being thrown at the world's problems keep falling short.

There is no utopia on the horizon.

Perhaps we are coming to terms with the oft-mentioned "myth of progress." N. T. Wright sums up this concept of hope while dismantling it thoroughly: "Modernism supposes that the world can become everything we want it to be by working a bit harder and helping forward the great march into the glorious future."[2] People thought (some still do) that with enough time and innovation, we humans would figure it out. We'd grow past our problems with science, education, and our overall awesomeness as humans.

This is, of course, quite prideful.

It has also proven quite foolish. Violence in the streets, an industry that keeps thinking of new ways to get pornography into your head and onto the phones of your children, wars with no end, a country that can't stop screaming at itself, active shooter drills, the still-existing scourge of slavery and hatred that fuels much of everyday life—all prove that we can't figure it out.

We are most definitely NOT evolving our way out of this.

And yet, we dream.

Against such a grim background, why can we not stop ourselves from visions of making a difference? To answer this question requires a bigger and better story. For you see, this itching urge to make things right comes from someplace deeper than you first imagined.

Let's now amend the cringe-producing sentence from a few paragraphs ago to something that points us in the right direction: *You were made to make a difference in this world.*

That's better.

WAKING UP THE HOBBIT IN YOU

I've never forgotten the connection author Ken Gire made years ago between the longings wedged deep in my soul and the simplest of Tolkien's stories.[3] Perhaps you've read *The Hobbit* (or at least watched the movies). In this less complicated, still grand tale of J. R. R. Tolkien's, the magician Gandalf hints early on of an adventure for our reluctant hero, Bilbo Baggins. "There is more to you than you know." Gire notes:

> He said this knowing that within the hobbit's veins
> coursed blood not only from the sedentary Baggins
> side of the family but also from the swashbuckling
> Took side.[4]

In some ways, Bilbo was made for this very moment that was now before him. Mind you, I'm not sure it had occurred to him until that day Gandalf invaded his home, followed by a band of pushy and uncouth dwarfs. The calm and predictable world of young Baggins was instantly disrupted by these strangers with insatiable appetites. With both his pantry and energies depleted, the overwhelmed hobbit finally collapsed by the fire to catch his breath.

That's when it happened.

The overstuffed visitors started singing, and the ancient melody filled this little hobbit's home while the words filled his heart.

"Then something Tookish woke up inside him, and he wished to go and see the great mountains, and hear the pine-trees and the waterfalls, and explore the caves, and wear a sword instead of a walking-stick."[5]

You may know of such stirrings.

It's a tug on your own heart when praying, a more-than-coincidence conversation you had this past week, the lingering phrase of a worship song, an injustice from which you cannot look away, or a truth from Scripture that echoes long after you read it.

A radical idea has now wedged itself into your thoughts: the Kingdom awaits. The love and power of God will soon invade this not-yet-healed world through little ol' you. Something new has awakened in you. And as strange as it sounds, you sense something strangely familiar about this longing.

Ah, now we are getting very close to the even bigger, true story of our beginnings.

THE *IMAGO DEI*

From Revelation, let's turn all the way back to the first book in our Bibles.

In Genesis we find the origin of a fledgling nation formed to bless the entire world. Starting in the twelfth chapter, we find the backstory of a storied people and their patriarch, Abraham.

Go back even further—into the primeval history of those earliest chapters—and we find the backstory of us all.

Philosophers and scientists alike speak of the origin of all things. Without a detailed explanation (which we couldn't fathom anyway), the opening lines of Scripture tell us the cause of it all.

In the beginning God created . . .[6]

Out of glorious love and infinite power, the eternal Father, Son, and Spirit created all that exists—the spectrum of light, the expanse of space, blazing galaxies we can barely see, and worlds we have never seen.

But oh, the world our eyes behold: skyscraping trees, paint-speckled wildflowers, sharp-edged canyons, and soft desert dunes. Rainforests teeming with life and oceans churning with color. Aardvarks and antiquarks, DNA and duck-billed platypuses, chinstrap penguins and the children who giggle at them.

God created it all out of his boundless goodness.

A LITTLE HEBREW GRAMMAR

Throughout those first exalted verses of Scripture are rhythmic echoes and refrains, circling 'round and always returning to the main character at the center of it all—the Eternal One.

And God said . . .

And God saw . . .

God . . . separated . . .

Without going into too much detail, there is a certain kind of verb form in Hebrew (the original language of Genesis) that is being used here to provide the rhythm. It is called the *weqatal* form, pronounced "vah-ik-tol" for the four of you who might be interested.

Linguists like Robert Longacre will tell you that a chain of these kinds of verbs is the backbone of Hebrew storytelling: the weqatal chain.[7] One of the scholars at our church[8] likens it to an excited adolescent telling a story: "*and so* then this happened, *and then* he showed up *and I* said *and she* said *and then* they left *and we* . . ."

You hear the rhythm and progress building throughout this majestic account of creation in the first chapter. But then it comes to a drastic and screeching halt midstory. Why?

To make a point.

It's like a song that keeps repeating and building on itself until it all stops suddenly. Then you hit the release, the pinnacle of the song (and back in the old days, a key change). Think back to that moment in a particular Whitney Houston song[9] when everything kept building up to that one dramatic moment and then it all stopped suddenly . . . and then . . . wait for it . . . two, three, four (big key change):

And I . . . will always . . . love you . . .

THAT's the moment everyone remembers, the pinnacle of the song.

THE "BRING US HOME, WHITNEY" MOMENT

The very same thing is happening in the poetry of Genesis 1. There is a rhythmic and repetitive crescendo in the description of what God has done. It's all happening with that unpronounceable verb form (*And God said . . . And God saw . . .*). And then it all comes to an abrupt stop. The chain ends. The band stops playing.

Where? Where is the drop out, hold-your-breath-because-it's-all-about-to-explode moment? The crest of the poem is verse 27:

So God created mankind in his own image . . .

Break in the chain . . . wait for it . . . two, three, four . . .

> in the image of God he created them;
> male and female he created them.

It's quite possible I'm not doing this justice, but what is the big key-change, "bring us home, Whitney" moment in the text? *In the image of God he created them; male and female.*

This is the pinnacle of creation's song.

AND NOW A LITTLE LATIN

It boggles the mind and bankrupts the vocabulary: Out of all God's magnificent creatures, we alone bear his image. To grasp the weight of this moment in the story is more than we can fully handle. But let's try as best we can with our limited abilities.

We have ways in which we uniquely resemble our Creator— our capacity for knowing and loving him, our creativity, our intellect, our embedded sense of justice, to name but a few. We are made from dust, but still, we are the capstone of creation— fashioned in the very image of God.

If you prefer it in Latin: the *imago Dei*.

Created in the image of our triune God, we are created for relationship—with each other and, in a distinct way, with God. The longings of our souls trace back to this innate capacity for intimacy with the Eternal One. Much has been rightfully written on this extraordinary truth.

But there is even more in the meaning of this image-bearing that separates us from all other creatures.

A STARTLING RESPONSIBILITY

When reading the dog-eared early pages of Genesis, we mustn't forget the wonder of that first audience. To appreciate the impact of bearing the image of God, it will help to remember the wisdom of authors Richards and O'Brien,[10] who wisely ask: How would those who first heard these momentous words understand such things?

Created in the image of our triune God, we are created for relationship—with each other and, in a distinct way, with God.

In the ancient Near Eastern world, a king or pharaoh was assumed to be the representative of some so-called god (note the lowercase *g*), and he ruled on behalf of that god. He was the visible representative of the "deity" in that corner of creation. Minus the pagan notion of many gods (which is consistently rejected in the Scriptures), could this cultural context offer another clue of how Genesis was first heard?

Yes. We are not gods, nor should we be treated as such. Never are we to dominate our world with crushing power like ancient monarchs and demand worship. None of this is God's way. Still, this first audience would've heard the idea of image-bearing to include *a certain kind of ruling*.

The plan all along was for us to represent the God of the universe in his creation. Of all creatures, we humans would have the best chance of reflecting his love and care to each other and the rest of creation. That's how that first audience would've heard this astonishing news and all its implications.

Again: We are to rule but never exploit.

In the second chapter of Genesis, it says that we are to *care* for creation,[11] a verb that is elsewhere translated as "guard."[12] So we protect and care in a way that reflects how God feels about his creation. Sadly, some have forgotten this part of our story. Others have now rushed to fill the void; caring for creation even as they ignore the Creator. We who champion the God of Genesis have been too silent and too inactive for too long.

We, of all his creatures, should celebrate this wondrous planet and the opportunity to care for it. This need not lead to bad theology. Christians can feel the weight of God's mandate without getting lost in the worship of his handiwork.

This is part of what it means to rule.

It is uncomfortable getting so close to the word *rule*, yet this is the stuff of which we are made, the cloth from which we are cut. Still, you're not liking this, some of you. And for legitimate reasons! Most have experienced firsthand the power-hungry and self-obsessed who think themselves God-appointed rulers. Some dare to hide their narcissism behind passages like this one. No wonder people are hesitant when it is suggested that we are somehow at the apex of creation, set apart as rulers.

The abuse of privilege and responsibility has left too many scars on too many fellow image-bearers and too many pockmarks on too much of the earth.

This is not his way.

The one true God wants you to know that you (yes, *you*) were created in his image, the image of Elohim,[13] the one who spoke it all into existence. ALL of us bear the dignity and weight of that authority. Not just the king. Not just those in power.

You are the royal representatives of the majestic and matchless LORD.

To bear his image is not only a statement of human dignity, it is a statement of human responsibility.

There is more to you than you know.

MADE FOR SOMETHING MORE

It is your turn to care. Guard. Bless. And yes, even create.

You will never chisel a mountain out of granite or paint a fiery sunset. You'll never curl the delicate eyelashes of a newborn. But your artistry still brings blessing and beauty into this world for the glory of God. You create a business and with that, economic opportunities. You turn around hopeless situations in a family, community, or team. You call out the greatness of students by the way you teach. You save lives by responding first to disaster. You protect the rest of us. You bring comfort. You feed, serve, clothe others. You clean up the planet. You sponsor someone in a support group. You encourage someone to take their own steps into this life with God.

Through it all, you guard the dignity of others and remind us to honor the image-bearers we walk among. You cultivate the chance for peace. With God's help, you create openings for grace to shine through. With each of these moments, God's world is a better place.

This is what God intended.

We are to work in such a way that we bring glory to him, bring order out of chaos, bring beauty into this world and shalom to each other. All the while honoring the God who has vowed to make things right in this no-longer-right world. It is the promise of Genesis and the love of Jesus. It is the hope of the gospel for tired hearts.

> With God's help, you create openings for grace to shine through.

This is why we keep dreaming— deep down, we know. It's why a man who barely knows Jesus is already making plans to tell others. Something is stirring inside. We were made to make a difference.

Anything less is settling for less.

Is such talk realistic? I think so—not to change the world on our own; we can't do that. No government, no educational system, no worldwide organization can fully remedy what's wrong with this world. No movement championed by your favorite famous person will do it. *We* can't do this on our own. Remember the myth of progress?

But as forgiven followers, dripping in God's grace and indwelt by his Spirit, we can get some things done in this world.

It is time to push back the Baggins part of us that, as Gire puts it, "wants to sit in its hobbit hole, safe and snug, with an inside latch locking out the dangers and uncertainties of the world beyond its door."[14] It's time to live with a completely different perspective on life. To step into the adventure with a God whose plan for you is as real as anything you've experienced. Why?

You were made for this.

And who knows, along the way, something Tookish might

awaken in each of us—under an overpass, just off a busy intersection of our own lives.

FOR PERSONAL REFLECTION

- Do you think God is still on the move in our world? What about in your own life? Why or why not?
- Where do you long to see God's presence in your world?

3
LIVING IN A VUCA WORLD

IN RECENT MONTHS, the jagged edges of this broken world left deep cuts in two families in our church. No, these were not the sensational and controversial stories that break the heart of an entire congregation. But for any who were close to either family, hearts were indeed broken. The jarring surprise of one; the howling injustice of another.

Such stories happen far too often. When they reach us as merely news, it leaves us saddened—from a distance. Our planet and all who inhabit it truly do need supernatural help. Such things are not right and not as God would have it.

When such a story lands close, we are staggered by the nearness of it: the pain, the confusion, the anger, and the questions. All this talk of planet-wide struggle has come home. It's all true and it's now become real. It is intensely personal.

Live long enough in this world and such a moment finds you—hopefully a lesser version, but still full of your own hurt and confusion. The question, then, is this: How does one live courageously in a world with such possibilities? How do we not fall back in defeat and discouragement? How do we not give in to settled cynicism?

The adventure of a difference-making life sounds grand, in theory. But how do things get done when the world beyond our latched door contains such "dangers and uncertainties"? It will require that completely different perspective previously mentioned.

To explain, I'll give you two big words and an even bigger thought.

THE FIRST BIG WORD IS *HONESTY*

It is intellectually dishonest and emotionally unhealthy to deny all that is happening around us. To put a blunter edge to it: There is a distinct difference between denial and faith. The life to which God calls you does not require eyes scrunched shut and minds closed off. In fact, just the opposite.

You see, we live in a VUCA world. What's VUCA? An acronym. You're familiar with acronyms. Depending on how old you are, you translate them without thinking. VHS, LP, and YMCA for the older among us. ICYMI, ELI5, and PAW for the younger. And for the nostalgic, perhaps you remember when people still went to malls to get some TCBY with their BFFs. We now live in a veritable alphabet soup of abbreviations. Some day in the future, archeologists will study the remnants of this language the way scholars study hieroglyphics of ancient Egypt.

Let's get back to the point ASAP.

VUCA is a term now used by "complexity scientists." Its origins reach back to the US Army War College describing the post-Cold War world in the late 1980s, but the word didn't come into widespread use until the wake of the September 11, 2001, terrorist attacks.[1] Here's what it stands for:

- Volatility
- Uncertainty
- Complexity
- Ambiguity

Take your pick of the four. With the hyperconnectivity of this age, we strain to keep up with an ongoing flood of information about a dizzying number of topics—from global crises to personal threats to ethical decisions we feel ill-equipped to make. Of course, not only knowledge comes rushing in but also a constant flow of shockingly loud opinions on everything we think, do, wear, eat, listen to, and yes, believe. Versions of news stories fly in from every angle, leading to a general distrust of them all. Young and old alike live in a constantly overwhelmed state of mind.

It's disorienting.

Like never before, we now appreciate this strange acronym.

How, then, can we live differently in such a place and still be fully engaged?

We will need a way of thinking that holds up to the unsteadiness of our times, a way of loving that heals the unkindness of our times, a way of believing that endures the fear of our times. A point of reference that orients us in these disorienting times.

It must be honest, for we will deal with the world as it is, not as we wish it to be. But there is more, for we will now respond to the world as God would, not as we sometimes wish he would. This will require us to pay attention to a very big thought.

As it turns out, there's a German word for this.

THE VERY BIG THOUGHT

Okay, the Germans seemingly have a word for everything. Which, I'm sure, makes it easier for them to talk to each other.

What I mean is they sometimes have a word that sums things up rather well.

Like this one: *Weltanschauung*. From this mouthful comes our word *worldview*: a comprehensive, take-it-all-in view of reality. So why use a three-dollar German word when a perfectly good English one is on the table? Because it seems to convey a serious consideration of the whole cosmos. It's a wide-angled perspective that defines how you approach everything. (Besides, for the briefest of moments, I sound smarter than I am.)

We all have a worldview, whether we think much about it or not. It's our perception of how things are, how they work, why they work (or don't). It's our take on what matters (and why).

You know what matters? Your worldview.

Why else would Paul stress such a thing in his magnum opus? After eleven of the most profound chapters in Scripture, the apostle turns toward the practical in the twelfth chapter of Romans. After all that theology, how are we to respond to the mercies of God? How are we to live life in this world as God would have us do?

> Do not conform to the pattern of this world, but be transformed by the renewing of your mind. Then you will be able to test and approve what God's will is—his good, pleasing and perfect will.[2]

What distilled wisdom lies here. What an answer to our wobbly ways.

- Do not allow the general drift of this world to pull you off course.
- Instead, yield to God's masterful sculpting. In J. B. Phillips's translation of this verse, it's worded: "Let God re-mould your minds from within."

- This always-renewing you will better distinguish God's way from the chaos around you.

To shock and soothe this world in all the right ways, we must first align our thinking with his. As we "test and approve what God's will is" in our everyday life *every* day, a wise and discerning way emerges. We continually train ourselves to neither shake our fists at the world God loves nor surrender our convictions for mere acceptance by that world.

Now we are resisting the patterns of this world even as we are shaped by God's influence, beginning to view things in light of his perspective.

Call it a worldview.

A SLOW FADE TO IRRELEVANCE

A joint study by Barna and Summit Ministries suggests those who call themselves Christians are experiencing a loss of that perspective: "only 17 percent of Christians who consider their faith important and attend church regularly actually have a biblical worldview."[3]

This definition of a "biblical worldview" is one Barna has used for decades and includes the basic beliefs of Christianity.[4] According to their research, the vast majority of Christians surveyed seem to have stirred in enough from other religions and competing worldviews to arrive at something less-than-orthodox—some without even realizing their perspective counters biblical truths.

So what?

Some might consider this the natural by-product of globalization and think that Christian leaders need to lighten up. I'll leave the various reasons for the above observation to others, but we shouldn't treat such a thing lightly. Why? Because a biblical worldview is an essential ingredient to the difference-making life Jesus calls us to. The life brimming with "hot" and "cold" requires clear, honest thinking tethered to the wisdom of God.

How does one "renew" their mind and consciously tend to this worldview?

A biblical worldview is an essential ingredient to the difference-making life Jesus calls us to.

You already know the answer. Fear not—for the rest of the chapter is not a guilt-inducing harangue about quiet times and reading your Bible through in a year (though both are well-tested strategies). Instead, notice how this very big thought only fits in the context of a very big story.

WHERE TO BEGIN

Steep yourself in the story. All of it. Even the uncomfortable twists, turns, and threads that aren't fully explained yet. Stay with it when you're frustrated or offended. Ask honest, humble questions of honest, humble Christians who are also finding their place in the story.

In this big thought of a biblical worldview, you will continually encounter a bracing honesty. This is the world as it is, not as we wish it would be. Issues encountered across all cultures and beliefs show up with regularity: the question of good and evil, the longing for justice, the need for mercy, the power of sacrifice, and the craving for significance, to name a few.

This view of reality does not explain away everything—that is where faith comes in. It's also where the thrill of being alive shows up. We learn. We wonder. We trust. And cry and fail and pray and find forgiveness. Prodigals return home. The proud humble themselves. The more fortunate share with the less fortunate. It is unpredictable in some details and perfectly consistent in others. But life matters in this greater scheme of things. There is a Creator calling us close to encounter him. To know him. This is awfully mysterious and terribly real.

To read the Scriptures is to meet a variety of people who often knew God in this way but rarely received all the answers to their questions about life in this world. They grappled with him *inside their faith*. This view of the world gave them not only meaning, but a framework in which they could keep asking, struggling, and seeking. What a gift this will now be in these uncertain times.

The questions show up in every faith.

The disquiet of a thoughtful soul is not unique to Christians. The world will accost you with its unanswered questions that twist and torture, no matter your faith. At least let us acknowledge this much. It is another intellectual sidestep to think only the Christian framework brings up such doubts and concerns—remember our VUCA world.

Ravi Zacharias says it so well: "We must recognize that every worldview can leave us with questions that we cannot exhaustively resolve this side of eternity. Every worldview has gaps."[5]

This is not a schoolyard tactic of pulling everyone down to the same level. "Oh yeah? Well your worldview has problems, too—so there." No. It is simply a logical and honest observation that must be made. No one gets through this life unscathed. All who live in this world long enough will have their fair share of burning questions. What makes the difference is, as Zacharias asserts, that the framework of Christianity is "far more adept" at dealing with some of these big and hairy questions.[6]

> All who live in this world long enough will have their fair share of burning questions.

So ask away.

If your faith is tumbling in doubt, say it out loud. Find other believers who won't run away in shock. If you are the one now listening to bothersome questions with no easy answers, please stay close. And curious. In my experience, there is usually something behind the initial question. Sift through it all together, remembering that you stand in a great tradition of those searching for God's answers inside their belief.

And keep returning to the story.

When someone does leave the faith, don't slam the door and lock it on their way out. No scorching tweets. No brimstone-laced messages. No gossipy whispers. Keep loving and listening well. Pray for the wisdom to know what to say and what NOT to say. Not yet. If we really believe God is still in the business of redeeming those he loves, that would include your friend. Keep praying, yes, and as much as possible, keep doing life together.

And keep returning to the story.

IT'S A LOVE STORY, NOT A RULE BOOK

Some questions are so big they will only fit in a very big narrative.

Hang around most churches for more than a verse of "Amazing Grace," and you'll hear someone quote Psalm 119:105: "Your word is a lamp for my feet, a light on my path." It's true. God longs to guide you through this life. His Spirit-breathed word has been protected and collated throughout the ages for this very purpose.

As such, there are significant claims and specific instructions throughout; guardrails intended to keep us from careening off the cliff. Approaching Scripture as merely a collection of commands misses the much bigger point, however. Firm and timeless guidelines exist, but approaching the Bible as merely a list of do's and don'ts reduces it to so much less than the eternal God intended.

This is the grand love story of our Creator and the world he refuses to abandon.

Writers call this the "arc" of the story. Think of it as the textured plotline stretching from beginning to end with all its twists, tragedies, heroes and villains, hopes, dreams, losses, promises, and triumphs woven together. All moving toward a completion, a resolution, or in French, "a denouement"[7]—the relief at the end that comes from untying the gnarled knot.

THE OTHER BIG WORD

In this very big idea of a biblical worldview we are informed, of course, by the story found in the Bible. It is refreshingly honest. But there's another word we need to survive: hope.

In addition to his important words on the "mighty long journey" toward racial reconciliation,[8] Professor Robert Smith Jr. has written much on preaching and living out what one dares to preach. His words carry weight for many who call themselves preachers.

In an interview about preaching, he stated, "I'm passionate about making the connection between 'fall' and 'future.'"[9]

We've acquainted ourselves with the story of Genesis and the heartbreaking moment sin entered the story. But that unleashed the chaos, sorrow, betrayal, and death that now touches us all. The jagged edges of this broken world trace back to the original rebellion. It is important we not ignore the truth we find in this part of the story.

Smith agrees, but he reminds us all that we must pair this grim truth with our future hope.[10] To tell the whole story means presenting the gloriously redeemed future state of God's people and the world he will restore for them.

By taking just a few steps back, the entire vista of Scripture reveals a stunningly passionate God actively engaged with his creation, restoring that which has gone horribly wrong. This redemption will find its way into every aspect and layer of existence in the cosmos. This is what God is up to, even now. This is the bigger backdrop of meaning that guides our steps and provides room enough to ask those big and hairy questions.

When it finally occurs to us that we've been summoned by God into this heroic tale of redemption, the Tookish part of us finally awakens. There is a unique role written for us in this epic plot. God is that big and that good and that mindful of us.

THE EPIC INCLUDES THE VERY PERSONAL

Some struggle with talk of having a "personal relationship" with Jesus, and to be sure, the phrase has become a spiritual cliché for many. As one of our church's young pastors[11] put it recently: It's not just praying a prayer, joining the club, and eating pizza. This is a different, ever-changing, spiritual life lived in the physical world.

> There is a unique role written for us in this epic plot. God is that big and that good and that mindful of us.

When Jesus said he'd be with us always, he meant that in a very real way. You experience him personally—that sounds mysterious, and it is. You begin to learn from him and yield to his way of doing things. As you soak your thinking in his Scriptures, you start seeing things as he does.

The process rarely unfolds in a linear, step-by-step manner; rather, it's a back-and-forth between you and the Lord of all. Then watch how he connects this to the rest of what he's doing with his people—past and present. The ongoing work by the Great Restorer is ultimately relational.

This is the renewing of your mind and the emergence of a new worldview.

Still, from where does courage arise? It is one thing to notice a Tookish longing to make a difference; it is quite another to move—with a resolute heart—into the heartache. What is the source of such hope? Such courage? How are we less likely to be lukewarm as we engage this world?

The story, of course. To be more specific: the turning point of the story.

It begins in Genesis, in a shalom-soaked garden that wasn't just good but *very good*. We know this is no longer true. We've admitted as much. The world must now be set to rights. This is the work of God, and it has begun: Into our sin-stained broken-ness came the King himself.

He is the turning point.

He is the source of our hope and courage.

This is the beginning of the beginning of everything new.

THE FINALE WE DESPERATELY NEED

I was reminded recently (by John Stonestreet and Brett Kunkle, in their very helpful book *A Practical Guide to Culture*[12]) of a scene in C. S. Lewis's *The Lion, the Witch and the Wardrobe*. What they could not know is how that scene and that story became entwined with the story of my parenting of two little girls. It is the pivotal moment where the great king, Aslan, sacrificed himself to the White Witch to redeem the traitor Edmund. It is a children's story, but for those who've read it, it is so much more. Over the course of almost countless nights, I would read from these chronicles until we had journeyed through all seven books. Paraphrasing off-the-cuff when necessary, employing all the voices I could find in my imagination, I introduced my young daughters to Narnia. There were giggles and gasps along the way. Long detours to explain things and consider important matters like how fun it would be if animals could talk. Like I said, these are stories for children.

And grown-ups.

For along the way, we met Aslan, the great king who just hap-pens to be a majestic lion. As the girls also noticed, he reminded them of an even greater King. Lewis would be pleased. And then came the night where we witnessed Aslan's great sacrifice for an undeserving boy. I read of his humble surrender to the evil forces that had surrounded him. I tried to get through the horrible taunts in ugly voices of my own making, and then there was the heart-shattering moment when the Great One laid down his life on the stone table.

I dared to peer over the edge of the book at two little girls, delicate tears now forming, pleading, "Daddy this can't be right; this is too sad a story." All the cheering of all the evil creatures who hated Aslan and his kingdom was almost too much. They were right. It is too sad a story. For my Alex and Tori, it appeared all hope was lost, for now the great king was dead.

What they desperately needed—and I was only too happy to offer—was the rest of this magnificent tale. You'll know, if you've read the whole story, the morning after that dreadful night, the sisters (in the story) heard a dreadful crack and turned to see the stone table on which Aslan had been killed now broken in two. But he was not there.

And then, a voice they knew. Somehow Aslan, who had died, now lived again. He stood before them. They wondered what it all meant—as did two other sisters.

> *"It means," Aslan said, "that though the Witch knew the Deep Magic, there is a magic deeper still which she did not know. Her knowledge goes back only to the dawn of Time. But if she could have looked a little further back, into the stillness and the darkness before Time dawned, she would have read there a different incantation. She would have known that when a willing victim who had committed no treachery was killed in a traitor's stead, the Table would crack and Death itself would start working backwards."* [13]

My girls could not have known all this phrase could mean, but they knew enough to recognize good news when they heard it. Death did not win. Evil did not have the last word. I'm not sure any of us fully appreciate what this means, but because of Jesus' death and resurrection, death itself will not win. The glorious power of God that emptied the tomb of Jesus will start working backward.

No, our failures and heartaches are not undone. Neither are they ignored or forgotten. They are grieved by our loving God and will one day be fully healed. So, too, this ruined and wondrous creation. At the greatest of cost, Jesus has wrested the story from the darkest of endings. Death and sorrow will not have the last word. Evil will not win. This is the beginning of everything new.

It has already begun.

When confronted with competing worldviews, none offer the brutal honesty and expansive hope of Scripture. Were it not for the main character of the story, this would all be sheer fantasy. Without the unique historical figure of Jesus and the reasonable evidence of his resurrection, it's just another story.

But with the credibility of Jesus, everything changes. A new world has opened up. We cannot see it all, but we know where the story is headed and what we are called to in the meantime. This is why we hope. This is why we worship. This is why we will not settle for less than the life Jesus intended for us.

Because of the Resurrection, the hope shimmers in the shadows even now, before that finale to end all finales. In the meantime, walk into this VUCA world with eyes wide open to the horrors and injustices that abound. Notice your own doubts and struggles. Admit them out loud.

Live like you believe the world has been invaded by the best life-giving news possible.

Then behold the bigger view of this world. Dive deeper into the Scriptures that await, and allow God to renew and refresh your thinking. Live like you believe the world has been invaded by the best life-giving news possible.

This is the story we find ourselves in.

FOR PERSONAL REFLECTION

- What steps can you take to surrender to Jesus and allow him to transform your mind?
- On the spectrum of hopeful to hopeless, where do you put yourself? Why?

4

THE REAL BAT CAVE

I'VE NEVER BEEN DEAD or even mostly dead.

No white lights at the end of the tunnel. Nothing even close. I do, however, like to think that I have a teeny, tiny sliver of an idea of what it means to walk out of a tomb.

Allow me to explain.

On the heels of work with some heroes of mine in India, a handful of my buddies and I made the short jump over to western Nepal. One day, we asked our guide and translator to help us find a little mountain village where we'd heard there was a bat cave. Not a Bruce Wayne sort of bat cave; *a real cave*. Sure enough, we found a dilapidated, parklike entrance announcing a "bat cave" nearby. It appeared we were the only people with any desire to see this attraction—perhaps our first clue of things to come.

Hadn't I seen this in a scary movie? We paid the entrance fee, where a local man, hovering nearby, asked quietly, "Do you want to see bats?" "Yes, please." We soon discovered he was offering—for a negotiated price—to take us on a little detour through an unmarked branch of this cave to more bats than we could imagine.

Deal.

Winding down a forest path, we came across the mouth of this cave, agape at the bottom of steep, decrepit steps—another eerie clue. With all of three flashlights hastily found and now distributed between the seven of us, we entered the cave. The ceiling, twenty or so feet above, felt comfortably high—strung with rudimentary lights. Then, as the marked, more touristic cave continued, our guide motioned for us to start climbing up a pile of rubble to the right, toward the ceiling of the cave.

It turns out there was an opening at the top of that heap. In retrospect, this other vein was likely revealed after one of the earthquakes that has shuddered through this region. The path now narrowed on this upper route as the ceiling lowered with each step. Soon, we "stood" at the entrance to the real bat cave, a black hole less than three feet high.

Laughing nervously as we mustered our courage, a British couple emerged from the darkness muttering something about it being "so dark." "Bats?" we asked. "Yes, yes, lots of them. We just need to get out of here." And with that, our team was down to six. One of our crew very much hates tight spaces, so he went back with the breathless couple.

Probably a good thing.

Without going into too much detail, we now crawled into the darkness single file, passing the lights up and down the line in spaces so tight I had to think creatively how to bend myself through the coiled capillaries of that mountain.

Eventually, the passage opened to a larger room. The ceiling was carpeted with fluttering, leathery wings, and we heard the nervous chatter of innumerable creatures resting above us. We dared not disturb them as we gasped for air.

Here's a fun fact: With many bats comes much guano (look

it up—I'm done explaining). This means the oxygen levels are lower in these tight, unventilated spaces. After a few more thrills (including a drop-to-the-floor moment when our host accidentally agitated the whole lot of them, inspiring several "God protect us from rabies" prayers), we eventually backtracked through the wormhole into the main cave and then, to the light beyond.

What does that have to do with anything?

Six men gulping every drop of oxygen from that thick air, darkness you could feel on your skin, and coffin-tight spaces with more than a few creepy crawlies. No one said it out loud, but our bravado hid a simmering unease. When we stepped back into the open air and blinding brightness, an almost giddy euphoria washed over us.

We sat at the only little general store in that village in the low mountains of the Himalayas and drank chai tea and ate everything they would sell us. We celebrated. We laughed and told inflated stories of our bravado. We reveled in the moment of our rebirth. The air was crisper, the light was more golden, and life itself tasted a little better in that moment.

It was like walking out of a tomb.

You don't have to slither into and out of a silly situation in Nepal to know what I'm talking about. This new life with God starts now—not in heaven someday. Fully alive and fully awake, we can breathe again. "I once was lost, but now am found": Isn't that how the former slave trader John Newton put it in his hymn "Amazing Grace"? "Was blind but now I see."[1]

That's it: *now I see.*

This may sound crazy, but when I came out of that hole in the earth, the snow atop the mountains seemed whiter, spackled against those heaping mountains. I remember looking into a valley a couple hours later, convinced it was more velvet than grass. I'm sure it was all there prior to our little venture into the dark, but still . . .

I saw what I had not fully noticed before.

I wish I could report I still see the world with such wonder. Unfortunately, my dulled vision has mostly returned. But who says we have to settle for such somber tones? Doesn't it make sense for those of us who have experienced a new life in Christ to see things more clearly?

SPIRITUAL VISION

In 2 Kings 6, we find a timely story. Israel had split into two nations—north and south; both are losing their way terribly. It's the 800s BC, just before prophets like Hosea and Amos and Micah and Jeremiah step onto the scene. It is the era of evil kings and the very occasional good one. Still, God has not given up on his people, on calling them back from the edge of disaster. Just before the time of our story, the famous prophet of old, Elijah, had battled a dark regime and won in spectacular fashion. But those days are over.

> Doesn't it make sense for those of us who have experienced a new life in Christ to see things more clearly?

It is now the time of his successor, Elisha.

The protégé with the similar name never missed a beat. With the power of God so supernaturally evident, he served the powerful and the poor, making a difference at home and abroad during his lifetime as he, too, proclaimed the truth of Israel's God.

When a neighboring king was warring with Israel, every raid he initiated was foiled by Israel's king. It was as if he had a way of knowing what would happen in advance. As it turns out, he did.

> Time and again Elisha warned the king [of Israel], so that he was on his guard in such places.[2]

The enraged king of Aram logically assumes he has a spy in his inner circle. His officers inform him not of a spy within the ranks, but rather a prophet in Israel who knows their plans. "Every move you make, every step you take, sire, he'll be watching you."[3] Okay, they didn't say that, but they certainly captured their boss's full attention with these words: "Elisha . . . tells the king of Israel the very words you speak in your bedroom."[4] It turns out there was no traitor. It was the all-knowing God informing Elisha, who then passed on the plans to the king of Israel.

You can imagine how this unnerved the king of Aram.

Once Elisha's location was discovered, a large military detachment encircled that city overnight. The next morning, Elisha's attendant wakes up and sees an army of horses and chariots surrounding them. In fear, he asks the prophet what they should do. "Don't be afraid," Elisha answers. "We've got them outnumbered." The look on that attendant's face is not recorded in Scripture, but I'm guessing he's wondering if the great man had lost his prophetic marbles.

And then this: "Elisha prayed, 'Open his eyes, LORD, so that he may see.'"[5]

We must never settle for anything less than this prayer. We, too, need our eyes opened. Of course, most of us assume we can see. So did Elisha's attendant. How else could he notice the threatening horde surrounding them that day? But he did not see as Elisha saw things, for he was blind to spiritual matters.

Spiritual blindness is a big theme across the pages of Scripture. The prophet Isaiah would later tell Israel they were blind to the role God had for them to play in the world.[6] In the New Testament, Jesus calls the Pharisees—a religious power group of the day—"blind guides," "blind fools," and "blind men."[7] Paul (who used to be Saul) was literally blinded by the radiant presence of Jesus and knocked off his high horse to illustrate his own spiritual blindness.

AN EPIDEMIC OF BLINDNESS

Many people do not see the eternal implications of our daily lives. Living in the right now is hard enough. And so, even with all the talk of "being spiritual," most people still live for the tangible. As Os Guinness puts it, "the modern world quite literally 'manages' without God."[8] He goes on to warn that even many professing believers are functioning in this world as "atheists unawares."[9]

In such a state, how much of life do we miss?

To follow Jesus is to step into a life that experiences more, not less. He once spoke to Nicodemus about earthly things and heavenly things as if both were real. Have our eyes adjusted to this other reality? To voyage out of the doldrums of the status quo, we must begin to recognize the happenings in the realm layered above, around, and beneath the three-dimensional reality we know so well.

Otherwise, we'll soon be scared and ensnared before the battle has even begun.

Go back to the story in 2 Kings. A man wakes up with morning responsibilities as he cares for Elisha. He assumes another day like the last—oblivious to the enemy, blind to the spiritual battlefield on which he stands. Is it possible that we do the same? We stay laser-focused on the chores and tasks of the day, never considering that "our struggle is not against flesh and blood, but against the rulers, against the authorities, against the powers of this dark world and against the spiritual forces of evil in the heavenly realms."[10]

> To follow Jesus is to step into a life that experiences more, not less.

The church often relegates these mysterious words to the "prayer warriors" and spiritually sensitive among us. Those who intercede for others, those who enter the spiritual fray first, seem to appreciate the words of Paul better than most. But he wrote that sentence for everyone in the church in Ephesus.

Hold this strange and almost intimidating truth in your thoughts.

Both the physical and spiritual realms deserve our attention. We stand in the midst of a war between light and dark, good and evil. Let's not be surprised by that. Nor can we live as atheists unawares, acting as if there is no opposition to what God wants done in this world.

UNDER ATTACK

The very minute you vow to live a large life for God, very real forces will set against you. If it makes you feel any better, they've always opposed you. But in your new resolve to follow Jesus into this world he loves, there will now come both the head-on attacks and the nagging distractions sneaking up from behind. From familiar temptations to old habits to new challenges—be ready.

Do not fall prey to an incomplete gospel that whispers of only easy times and full bank accounts. Jesus told us otherwise. He said there'd be trouble.[11] (I do so love him for telling me the truth.) Some of that trouble is of our own making and some of it is thrown at us out of nowhere. And some of it is best understood as an attack by dark forces. Don't be surprised.

Neither should you recoil in fear.

Instead, live in the tension of two truths:

1. There are forces in this world that seek to destroy all that God loves.
2. There is a God greater than any such forces.

First John 4:4 (NASB) is a good verse to memorize here: "Greater is He who is in you than he who is in the world."

We'll see this play out in Elisha's story as well. For now, it is important to remember *our struggle is not against flesh and blood* and to keep such truth in perspective. As C. S. Lewis frames the discussion in his introduction to *The Screwtape Letters*, most people prefer to either ignore the forces of evil altogether or to take an unhealthy interest in everything demonic, which can be just as bad in the long run.[12]

It's better to see all that is happening and remember who gets the last word.

SEEING HALF THE EYE CHART ISN'T ENOUGH

Lewis suggests an approach to spiritual warfare that avoids getting stuck in the extremes, instead encompassing the entire spectrum of reality. Could this not apply to all of life? For various reasons (including those who imprinted their ways upon us growing up, our own bent toward personality, and the traumas and triumphs etched on each heart), we will trend one way or the other: Some people will see mostly the good. Others will see the bad. Some will see the opportunity first, others the threat. This is nothing new, and such broad-stroked statements merely stoke the conversation at parties. But instead of seeing a glass half full or half empty, which side of the eye chart do you focus on?

E		1
Injustice	Beauty	2
Rebellion	Restoration	3
Brokenness	Healing	4
Setbacks	Victory	5
Enemy	Champion	6

The key to the vibrant and robust life is to see and admit the whole truth.

Too often we drift to one extreme or the other rather than acknowledge both.

THE PRIVATE STRUGGLE FIRST

Never is this more evident and essential than on the battleground of our own hearts. With only half a truth in view, our enemy has more than enough to use our blindness against us. Take, for instance, the term *self-aware*, which has found its way into the modern vernacular. Usually we use it in a sentence to "help" the poor souls around us. As in, "God love him, if only he were more self-aware." (The "God love him" part is a dead giveaway to all that helpfulness.) Rarely do we pray or wish for our own self-awareness. Why? Because we have plenty, thank you very much. But do we? Here's a basic truth for each of us:

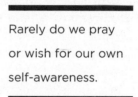

Rarely do we pray or wish for our own self-awareness.

The first rule of self-awareness is you're not.

At least fully. Rarely do you encounter someone who says, "I don't have a clue how I'm doing." Instead, we all know someone who keeps stumbling into the same old ditches, asking the same old questions: *Why does this keep happening to me? Why does that one thing always trip me up?*

Sometimes, instead of questions, blaming words scatter the responsibility outward: *The reason I'm in my eighteenth relationship is . . . The reason I keep moving from church to church is . . . The reason I'm so angry all the time is . . .*

You get the idea.

By the way, did you notice I couched all those examples as problems *other people* might have? You and I would never do that, would we? Again, the first rule of self-awareness is we're not.

THE DREADFUL TRUTH

Blindness to my own failures is more than a frustrating character flaw: It proves deadly to the soul. In a more expansive treatment of 2 Kings 6,[13] Timothy Keller suggests that we are blind to the depths of our sin. Part of my improving spiritual vision begins on this much more private level—the shocking moment my sin comes into full view.

There may be no better example of this than the prophet Isaiah. His vision of the exalted King of heaven (described in Isaiah 6) was so overwhelming and unsettling, it left this eloquent wordsmith with a three-word response: *Woe is me*. Why the overwhelming dread? He tells us:

> Woe is me! For I am lost; for I am a man of unclean lips,
> and I dwell in the midst of a people of unclean lips; for
> my eyes have seen the King, the LORD of Hosts![14]

Isaiah was not only confronted with the glory of the Eternal One, but in light of such glory he saw his own defilement. This makes sense, doesn't it? If God is more than we imagined, wouldn't our sin matter more to him?

Woe is me! For I am lost.

While Isaiah's initial reaction is essential to a larger life with God, such vulnerability fills us with a kind of primal fear—*If I admit this out loud to God or anyone else, I will be abandoned. I'm not worthy of relationship or community or anything, in light of my own wretchedness.* The fear of what one writer calls the "catastrophic collapse of relationship"[15] now rushes to the forefront.

Beware "the father of lies," as Jesus once called him,[16] whose whispers grow louder at this point. Even as you begin noticing and lamenting your own unclean ways, the forces of evil will subtly work against you. Satan, also called "the Accuser,"[17] will now push those admitted failures in your face. He doesn't care about your true sorrow; he's attempting to use it as a weapon against you. For the sake of our discussion, think of it as an attempt to blot out half your field of vision. Once you acknowledge the blight of your sin, the enemy will quickly try to make sure that's all you can see.

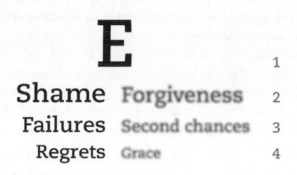

E	1
Shame Forgiveness	2
Failures Second chances	3
Regrets Grace	4

This new self-obsession with my failure can blind me as much as my denial of it. For me personally, when my shortcomings loom so large, I settle for self-doubt and distraction, if not full-on despair. What, then, is the way out?

Depending on the nature and depth of the failure, the important and personal work of the Holy Spirit will flow through various means: in private prayer, the help of trusted friends to whom we confess, or perhaps a Christ-following counselor. But the point remains the same.

You'll need the whole truth.

SEEING THE REST OF THE TRUTH

In his book the *Soul of Shame*, psychiatrist Curt Thompson details, quite remarkably, the anatomy of our shame and the need for these moments of stark vulnerability. But it cannot stop there. Such vision is only half of the truth. He writes: "Lurking deep within us is what Satan convinced our first parents to believe—that we are not important enough for God to remain with us."[18]

It is an old and pernicious lie.

We are that important, though not for any reason we can ever generate. We matter because we matter to the God whose image we bear. And for his own sovereign reasons, we are worth loving and redeeming. This is the marvelous gift of grace. You even see it in the vision of Isaiah. Just two verses after his woeful confession, the penitent prophet is cleansed: "Your guilt is taken away and your sin atoned for."[19]

Isaiah the sinner becomes Isaiah the redeemed, but only by an act of sheer grace.

This is how we survive the dreadful awareness of who we are: We see the rest of the truth. When the cross looms large, both my sin and the length to which God went to cover it are in plain view.

From the intense and intimate space of my heart, the same truth now begins to unfurl across the rest of my life. Like Isaiah, I'm now eager to consider how this plays out in the larger context of what God is still up to in the story. I've seen his power at work in my own life; surely it can happen elsewhere.

Here I am, send me![20]

THE CHALLENGE AND THE CHAMPION

Elisha's attendant woke up one day and smelled some pretty strong coffee: an entire army surrounding the city, there to destroy his friend. His reaction? Anxiety. Panic. Hopelessness. *Oh no! What shall we do?* He only saw the threat, not the triumph.

Elisha, however, saw all that was before him that day. You would expect him to know an army was coming—his source for information being quite reliable. Elisha was realistic and sober-minded about the encircling danger. That's part of opening your eyes. But he also saw the presence of his deliverer. That's why he told his frightened friend, *"Those who are with us are more than those who are with them."*[21] He never denied the presence of his enemy. He simply saw that those troops were outnumbered.

And then a gracious request for his befuddled companion: "Open his eyes, LORD, so that he may see." This is the prayer we must pray for ourselves and each other. Every day. Many times throughout our days.

May we see clearly the challenge before us *and* the champion who is for us.

A SIGHT TO BEHOLD

Try to imagine it—the hills surrounding this village are blanketed with the dust of stirring horses and creaking chariots. Flashes of sunlight bounce off the swords of eager soldiers, all there for one unarmed prophet. To most eyes, the battle is over before it even begins.

Then the man of God prays, and his friend's eyes blink open to the rest of reality: Ringed 'round the restless troops are warriors of light, angels of an army dispatched by the Lord of hosts. Chariots of fire dot the hills standing guard, ready to do God's bidding.

May we see clearly the challenge before us *and* the champion who is for us.

It's true. The battle was over before it began.

Are you starting to get a sense of how this spiritual vision works? You will begin to see that which was always there, but you had never noticed. There will be times God gives you courage because you'll see for the first time—or the first time in a long time—that you're not alone. A text from that friend who is praying at just the right moment. A Scripture verse wherein you see what God is saying to you. It could be a door slightly opened, an energy renewed, a vision reborn, some tiny sliver of hope.

Or it might just be the breathtaking beauty of God's handiwork, reminding you of his awesome power. *Whatever I face, wherever He sends me, I am in the hands of the Almighty God who did THAT . . .*

When I came out of that cave, for just the briefest of moments—minutes, or hours at best—my eyes saw things differently. Cobalt blues, cinnamon reds, and emerald greens I don't remember seeing before.

When you walk out of a grave, you see differently.

A TRULY JUMBO SHRIMP

If you remember your high-school biology, the human eyeball (the retina, specifically) is equipped with particular cells, called cones, which sense and interpret color. We have three different types that determine the color we see. Don't worry, none of this will be on the final exam. Just remember: More types of cones means more colors.

Since it was first broadcast, a particular episode of the Radiolab podcast has stirred up much conversation about colors.[22] To summarize, they began to ask the question: If a dog, a butterfly, and a shrimp (among others) looked at the same rainbow, would they see different colors?

Of course, to a large extent, we really don't know, since none of those creatures can communicate directly with us. But the conclusion of the various scientists contributing to that episode was "yes." For instance, your dog has color-receptive cones for two colors as opposed to three, which means his rainbow would have various shades of blue, green, and a touch of yellow. Compare this to the vibrant seven colors most humans see in the rainbow.

A butterfly, however, has five types of cones, which means the color combinations are beyond what we can see or imagine. This pales in comparison to the mantis shrimp, which is one of

God's truly intriguing creations. It can grow up to a foot long and looks like it swam through a tub of rainbow sherbet. It also packs one of nature's most powerful punches, often knocking out its prey.

This aggressive little crustacean has sixteen cone types in its odd little eyes. Some people might wonder if it could see a massive spectrum of color for which we have no words. I say "could" because other researchers have since suggested[23] there is more to seeing colors than types of cones—like how big your brain is and how much it can process.

That's okay. I don't want to be something that goes well with cocktail sauce anyway.

I do like to think that in eternity God will open my eyes up to all the colors he created as I take in the wonder of creation fully healed. Maybe this little detour into the anatomy of eyeballs is a coming attraction for the redeemed and restored universe. What is it Paul wrote? "What no eye has seen, nor ear heard, nor the heart of man imagined, what God has prepared for those who love him."[24]

NEW CREATURE, NEW EYEBALLS

Until then, I am a new creation and so are you. I'm going to go out on a colorful limb and say that as new creatures in Christ, we already have new eyeballs. No, we cannot see it all yet. Compared to what's coming, it's like looking through a veil, a mirror darkly.[25] But we still see enough with our grace-healed eyes that a deeper reality comes into view. Let's behold all of it.

Some of what God will show us is breathtakingly beautiful, some decidedly less so.

The fractured shalom of this world leaves enough heartache that you'll be tempted to look away, to dull your vision, to not be bothered by it all.

Now see it all.

Before you saw only the silhouettes of human trafficking, now you see a face. When someone is bullied online, you notice the name of a real person being hurt. The weary burden of poverty is not theoretical when you welcome a family into your life. Racism mourned from a distance is now more personal through the eyes of a friend.

Sometimes the blindness is healed in an instant, sometimes in stages. Like the man Jesus healed in Mark 8, at first we see people as blurry shapes and trees. But eventually we see the *imago Dei* in each of them.

Take it all in. The horrible and the almost hidden. When you allow the living God to awaken your soul and open your eyes, spiritual realities break into view, and some of them will break your heart.

But don't stop there.

Feast your eyes upon the splendor of our great God at work.

Behold the power of the Resurrection unleashed in the here and now.

The freedom of forgiving someone . . . the shocking joy of answered prayer . . . a gentle word truly turning away the harsher one . . . you see it now: the whole world teeming with these dead-coming-to-life opportunities. Look closely and see not just the heartache, but the healing. Not only the enemy at work, but our greater champion.

I've never once seen angels in chariots of fire. But I am learning to notice the miraculous power of God. With his help, on a good day, my vision is better. When you walk out of a grave, you see things differently.

Still, even with better vision, do we humans stand any chance of *really* making a difference?

Yes. A thousand times yes.

FOR PERSONAL REFLECTION

- Think back on your day. How did you get bogged down by the "chores of the day" and fail to notice the ways that God was actively working around you?
- In what area of your life do you wish you were more self-aware?

5

CHOOSE YOU THIS DAY

AFTER THE GREAT PROPHET MOSES, it was Joshua who led the fledgling nation of Israel into their future. When we arrive at the end of his story, the old general gathers the people at Shechem, the ancient city of the hill country. Here, where so many stories began, Joshua calls the people to a new beginning with God. He announces (again) his own decision to serve the God of Israel. And then he encourages the people to do the same. He knows them well. Time and again, often with recent miracles in the rear-view mirror, the children of Israel would forget the faithfulness of God and go their own way.

Joshua thus paints very clear options before a nation standing at a crossroads: Choose between following the so-called gods everyone around you chases or the true and trustworthy Yahweh. The decision was theirs. One scholar put it like this: "So we find throughout the entire book of Joshua an emphasis on choice—choice that makes a tremendous difference in history—for individuals, for groups, for future generations."[1]

As it was in ancient Israel, so it is again.

It is time for conscious choices to be made. Some of them public, like Shechem. Some so private and seemingly overshadowed by the grand saga, you might assume them insignificant. They are not. Like the people in Joshua's day, decisions made at these intersections define our days, our lives, our legacies. Will you settle for the mundane or follow the true and trustworthy one into the grand story?

Choose for yourselves this day whom you will serve.[2]

In Revelation 3, Jesus presents a similar choice to the Christians at Laodicea.

MORE BLUNT WORDS

[Jesus said,] "You say, 'I am rich; I have acquired wealth and do not need a thing.' But you do not realize that you are wretched, pitiful, poor, blind and naked."

REVELATION 3:17

Beneath that lukewarminess in Laodicea a familiar thought lurked: *I will need Jesus when I die, but not too much of him before then.* Of course, no Jesus follower in their right mind ever confesses such thoughts aloud. We do, however, tolerate early stages of this madness.

We whittle out the uncomfortable passages from our Bibles. Rationalize our way out of loving community. Cut corners on our business ethics. Blur lines on our sexual boundaries. Ignore those in need. Spend as we please. We still pray, but only about our agenda. Little by little, we take back our life from the God who paid everything for it.

These are the echoes of Laodicea, for they, too, had forgotten one shockingly obvious and sadly forgotten truth:

You need Jesus right now, not just in the veiled glory of eternity future.

The words following the picturesque image of a nauseated Jesus pack a similar jolt when the context is again noticed. We now know this city at its own crossroads did not have good water, but here are three things they did have:

1. A thriving banking industry (and economy). In AD 60, for instance, this area was destroyed by an earthquake. They rebuilt it on their own, with no financial aid from Rome.

2. A famous medical school and a specific treatment for eye diseases called "Phrygian powder."[3]

3. It was known for clothing production—in particular, items made of black wool from sheep grown in their valley.[4]

Among other things, the citizens of Laodicea considered themselves well-off, well-known for healing sight problems, and well-dressed with that beautiful wool.

Even without their famous eye powder, you can see the irony: They believed themselves above God's help.

Talk about a lack of self-awareness. It never occurred to this church how far they'd wandered. Cutting through their ignorance are words from Jesus meant to shock and sting: "You do not realize that you are . . . poor, blind and naked."

Could such a thing ever happen to us?

Only all the time.

IT CAN'T BE MY FAULT

In the 1700s, there was a disease called puerperal fever.[5] Childbed fever. Women would give birth and die within a couple days. In some hospitals, the mortality rate was as high as 70 percent. Some physicians began investigating the cause of such deaths.

One Hungarian doctor, Ignaz Semmelweis, compared two maternity wards—one with midwives and one with doctors. The one where doctors delivered the babies was losing five times as many mothers. Was it different delivery positions? No. The priest ringing a bell when someone died? No. (Remember, scientific knowledge was limited.)

Eventually, he noticed the same thing a physician in the US was discovering: The only noticeable difference was that doctors were performing autopsies, while midwives weren't. In those days, such things were not the work of a specialist. Thus, the same doctors doing autopsies in the morning would deliver babies in the afternoon—*without washing their hands*.

(Isn't it interesting how such a simple act of hygiene still saves lives?)

In their defense, no one had any concept of germs yet. Nevertheless, there seemed to be a connection between the morgue and the delivery room. Semmelweis ordered his staff to wash their hands with chlorine—merely because it effectively got rid of the smell of the autopsy. And with that, the rate of death dropped dramatically.

Good news? Not exactly.

Doctors were incensed with the suggestion that THEY were part of the problem. Unfortunately, Semmelweis wasn't very tactful in his interactions with fellow doctors, making enemies along the way. His counterpart in the US encountered the same reaction. It would be years before people realized that by merely washing their hands, lives would be saved.

Are you and I any different? What is your reaction to the uncomfortable truth, as Simon Sinek says, that "sometimes you're the problem"?[6]

The previous chapter challenged us, in moments of self-awareness, to not ignore the rest of the truth. With a growing awareness that invention and innovation cannot solve humanity's problems, a new thought emerges. In true human fashion, some rush to the other extreme, suggesting we *are* the problem, a living scourge on the surface of this blue-green jewel of the galaxy.

AN OVERREACTION THAT'S JUST AS WRONG

Filmmaker Jonathan Nolan explained the thinking behind his dystopian view of the future in HBO's controversial sci-fi series *Westworld*. When asked why humans are depicted as "broken . . . selfish creatures" who are unable to change, Nolan responded, "there's a flaw in our code and it follows us around."[7] The implication in the discussion is that humans almost deserve to be replaced by robots.

Here again, a nugget of truth is buried in the false conclusion. Dust this broken world for fingerprints, and you'll discover ours all over the crime scene. This much is undeniable. If you assume a solution will come from those who created the mess, then the end looms for humanity and maybe the planet—or so the thinking goes. Nolan is not alone in this pessimism.

The cultural shift toward such despair is easily observed in the avalanche of movies depicting a future overrun by robots, zombies, or viral outbreaks (take your pick) in a wasteland of our own making. Whatever the bleak tomorrow brings, blame the humans.

So much for being enamored with the myth of progress.

The conclusion is incorrect, yet we mustn't ignore a truth buried in that hopelessness. It will be an important clue to the difference-making life that is so clearly different.

Are Nolan's observations about a "flaw in our code" that far from Paul's in Romans 7? "I know that nothing good dwells in me, that is, in my flesh. For I have the desire to do what is right, but not the ability to carry it out."[8] Perhaps not. In less geeky terms, Scripture clearly asserts our code is flawed. Our nature does indeed work against us at times.

The history of our species reveals a lingering and persistent dark side. But let's read the whole story to see all of the truth. To allow N. T. Wright to complete a thought from a previous chapter: "The myth of progress fails because it doesn't in fact work . . . and because it underestimates the nature and power of evil itself."[9]

As before, it is important to speak aloud of evil.

RUINED AND IN THE RUINS

Evil poisoned creation through the sin of our first parents and continues to wreak havoc through our own rebellion. God was betrayed, and he will not be mocked. He warned of consequences, and soon they came. The specter of death, in all its forms, is everywhere.

The entire story is now littered with tales of us fighting each other, ourselves, and the God who loves us so.

We bear the image of the one true God, but our rebellion has marred us. Francis Schaeffer referred to humans as "glorious ruins;"[10] glorious in our likeness to the Creator, but ruins of what we once were. We are ruined and living in the ruins of a world that was once so much more.

Such a confession sobers the mind, but it need not crush the heart. Why? Come back to the story (again). It does not end with epic failure. God has not given up on his beloved. Wright continues:

Only in the Christian story itself . . . do we find any sense that the problems of the world are solved not by a straightforward upward movement into the light but by the creator God going down into the dark to rescue humankind and the world from its plight.[11]

THE HELP WE NEED

There it is again. The supernatural help we need. What else could explain the apostle Paul, just a few paragraphs after confessing our terribly flawed code, penning these words: "*In all these things we are more than conquerors.*"[12]

What happened between the despair at the end of Romans 7 and the triumph at the end of Romans 8? Well, technically, the entire eighth chapter. In the glorious heights of Paul's God-inspired words in those verses, God's remedy emerges. That's what happened. Those whose hearts fill with despair at the wreckage left behind our selfish ways are correct. But

> God has not given up on his beloved.

there is more truth to notice. We cannot stop with our "flawed code." Admitting our plight, we now cling to the rescuer. Never stop at Romans 7 when the eighth chapter awaits.

There is no condemnation for those of us who are in Christ Jesus. The very Spirit of God has taken up residence in us, whispering to us the truth of our adoption by Abba, our Father. Who can bring a charge against me when Jesus has died in my place? Go back and read it again and again. This is the heart of God revealed and the promise of life with him now. We are not alone, certainly not perfect, but adopted and protected and empowered.

This is the good news of the gospel.

Why, then, do we settle for stilted and stunted lives? Why are we oftentimes our neighbors' best excuse for ignoring the offer of life with God? Why am I as susceptible to this less-than-full life as anyone else?

No one intends to live in Laodicea; instead, we end up there one misstep at a time. Habits drift slowly and subtly back to lukewarm waters. But these are decisions we make to manage our lives without God's influence.

Somehow, we begin to overlook the God of blazing brilliance

and glory.[13] "Thanks God, but I'll take it from here." We may still try to do a decent thing every now and then, but on our own, empty of purpose and power.

Lukewarm.

What, then, is the way out?

UNDER HIS INFLUENCE

Over the course of the remaining chapters, specific results and reactions will affirm we are indeed moving away from Laodicea, not toward it.

None of it will happen by accident.

Difference-making never "just happens." It is the result of choices you make again and again. This is not merely a "do something" mentality (though action must be taken). The way out is a conscious act of relying on the Spirit of God. This is how he will lead you further away from lukewarminess.

From the searing truth of Scripture, to godly friends, to his personal influence in the deep and private spaces of my being, my only hope out of stagnation is to follow his lead.

> Difference-making never "just happens." It is the result of choices you make again and again.

You are called to have a lasting effect on the world around you, but this only happens as God has such an effect on you.

Back in Romans 8, Paul tells us that there are those who have set their minds on the old ways, the self-centered desires, the flawed code, as it were. We already know where this leads. But there are those who have set their mind on that which the Spirit of God desires. This is the way out, and we must *set our mind* on it.

Choose to ask for his help.

And then this: Ask for his power.

This is life under the influence of the same life-giving Spirit of God that raised Jesus himself from the dead.

> And if the Spirit of him who raised Jesus from the dead is living in you, he who raised Christ from the dead will also give life to your mortal bodies because of his Spirit who lives in you.[14]

The presence of God that breathed life into the universe is now "in" me? Yes, closer than your next breath. For some, this is a strange concept, because they're still trying to fit all of this into a merely physical universe. Admittedly, our words will now fail to fully sketch out a life lived with the indescribable God. Our limited vocabulary reaches only so far into the mystery.

Remember, there are other layers of reality that are just as real, just as vivid, and (here's a word I didn't make up) just as *experienceable*. We can and do experience God as close and private and powerfully near.

INGRAINED INTIMACY

The capacity for such intimacy was ingrained in us from the beginning.

Paul is describing something so engulfing, so powerful, and so exactly what we need. By the sheer love and transcendent sacrifice of Jesus, we who turn to him in humble, desperate, childlike, God-given faith are now welcomed into the family. We are forgiven, yes, but we are now on our way to being fully restored. And the hard-to-describe but even-harder-to-deny reality is that God is so near, so a part of your existence now, that the only way to express this is to say that the Spirit of God is "in" you.

When this awareness seeps into the cracks and crevasses where fear and doubt and lingering rebellion hide, things begin to change. It turns out, God is interested and involved and completely present in my thought life, my public life, my behind-closed-doors life . . . all of it.

The psalmist had it right (of course): "God is our refuge and strength, an ever-present help in trouble."[15] But why wait for trouble to reach out?

Ask for his help. Ask for his power.

From here, there is no formula or step-by-step process. Instead, it is a step of obedience followed by the very next step. What that looks like in your life is, in some ways, unique to the current terrain of your life. But our sovereign God is up to the challenge. He's ready for this journey out of lukewarminess.

ARE WE THERE YET?

Every parent has heard this question. Every child has asked it. We're still asking it: *Are we there yet?*

No.

The way out of this tepid existence is possible. But we will never get "there" if we don't start somewhere.

Even when the life we long for looms on the far horizon, some will be tempted to dismiss it because it is just that: on the *far* horizon. "It's too late for me." "It's too much work." "I wouldn't even know where to begin."

Beware of such whispers swirling in your head. The father of those lies is still at work, beckoning you back to the monotone and impotent. He cannot separate you from the love of God, but he'll do all within his power to keep you from living fully alive. One effective strategy is to overwhelm us into inertia.

For those who are stuck, for anyone who is tired or discouraged or frustrated, for all who need a little jump start, I'll give you a hint: The life you want will not happen all at once. But it will not happen at all if you never start.

So start.

Small.

In 2014, US Navy admiral William H. McRaven offered ten lessons he learned from basic SEAL training when he spoke at a college commencement.[16] He became a YouTube sensation when he said these words: "If you want to change the world, start off by making your bed."

His point is well-made. "If you make your bed every morning, you will have accomplished the first task of the day . . . it will encourage you to do another task and another and another." This is me now—the civilian nonSEAL—talking, but I think he is speaking of the momentum we all want in life. Especially when we're stuck. It becomes nearly impossible to imagine such a thing in the doldrums of a lukewarm existence.

> The life you want will not happen all at once. But it will not happen at all if you never start.

There is wisdom here for the rest of us nonSEAL types.

You start each day with certain choices that will set up the rest of your day (and your life). When we read the Bible, we come across very specific decisions in the middle of the blockbuster storylines: Moses went over to the burning bush. Ruth stayed with Naomi. Lydia hosted Paul. These were intentional choices. We sometimes burn too much energy pursuing the dramatic moment worth posting online, but it's the little ones that define a life. Pile up enough of them, and that's what you get—a life.

A life of significance will not appear out of thin air. That's not how things work. Whether you're new in your faith or stuck in your old faith, you will rarely find yourself saying, somewhat startled, "Why looky here! I am now wise in the ways of the Lord."

That's not how progress works in any other area of your life, is it? Have you ever awakened one morning, stepped on the scale, and exclaimed, "Hey, where did those fifteen pounds go? They were just here . . ." Alas, but no. Neither will you wake up tomorrow debt-free or a concert pianist. Oh, there are still moments when the outrageous generosity of God rains down on your life in ways you don't deserve. You know what we call that? Grace. It is the sheer grace of God, and we live by it every day.

A life of significance will not appear out of thin air.

This deeper life, where *you know that God is up to something*, rarely appears spontaneously, however. It requires an intentional move on your part. He's closer than you remember, and he's ready. Refuse right now to settle for less than what God is offering. It's a choice you'll make again and again.

What if you have drifted way off course?

Where *do* you begin?

THE STEP WE ALL MUST TAKE

Repent. That's your very first grace-aided decision. Look now at the rest of Jesus' words in Revelation 3: "Those whom I love I rebuke and discipline. So be earnest and repent."[17]

What sounded harsh was always motivated by love. Jesus loves me so much that he doesn't give up when I do. In the middle of a mess I made, my all-knowing Savior sifts through those circumstances and works in my life and with me (if I'll let him) to lead me out of Laodicea. He knows what I'm made for. It is the same for you.

He also knows we'll never get there until we stop heading down the wrong path.

Stop. Turn back now. In the Greek, that entire phrase suggests an urgency to this decision. Do not wait until your life is a little more organized. Do not wait until tomorrow, the end of this chapter, or the end of this book.

Unlike all those nineteenth-century doctors, own up to your

actions. By the way, this is so much easier for me to write down than to live out. There are moments when all I can muster is "God, help me to even get to the place where I can confess this aloud to you." Even that is a start. I'm admitting how desperately I need him. Often, it's a not-very-impressive, stumbling step. Yet it is the step we all must take. As Lecrae puts it in his bold autobiography:

> If you don't know you're lost, you can't be led. And if you can't be honest, you can't be healed. Before I could be rescued, I needed to realize I was stranded.[18]

RSVP

Get invited to enough dinners, parties, or weddings, and you'll recognize those letters. Répondez s'il vous plaît, or in plain ol' English: Please reply. Please respond to this invitation. It's hard to imagine the Lord God of the universe humbling himself with such a request, but at the end of this stern talk with the Laodiceans, Jesus puts the RSVP to end all RSVPs.

> Here I am! I stand at the door and knock. If anyone hears my voice and opens the door, I will come in and eat with that person, and they with me.[19]

If you'd just open the door . . . there's a debate among some scholars whether Jesus is talking to his own or to those who do not follow him yet. I happen to believe there's enough truth here for each of us. If you have accepted this gift of grace, if you look to Jesus alone—the crucified and resurrected Lord—for your rescue, then even now, there will still be moments you need to repent. To turn back from the lukewarminess of it all.

Please respond.

Do something about the dissatisfaction rumbling deep inside. Be intentional. Step back into community. Make the appointment.

Write the note. Start praying again. Reaquaint yourself with the voice of Jesus in the Gospels. Camp out in the eighth chapter of Romans.

Notice one more time what Jesus says to the Laodiceans:

For the spiritually impoverished: Stop settling for nickels and dimes when you can have Jesus.

For those covered in shame: Let Jesus cover you with his righteousness.

For those who cannot see what God is up to: It is now time to let Jesus open your eyes.

Now make a hard-nosed choice, just one (remember, even the small ones add up). Make your bed, so to speak, and watch what happens. And then do it again.

And for those of you who have not yet turned to Jesus? Please respond.

A NEW WAY

Understand that this verse isn't a set of words that magically make things all better. Remember, the "coming in" language is describing a rich and very personal experience. What is specifically being described here would sound very intimate indeed to a first-century audience. As author Daniel Akin explains in *Exalting Jesus in Revelation*, "In the Middle Eastern world, an invitation to share a meal was characteristic of hospitality and the occasion for intimate fellowship with family and close friends."[20]

To share a meal in a home is an honor. It is the comingling of lives, the place of laughter and tears, of stories and hopes. It is where vulnerability flourishes in safety. These are the trappings of relationship, and you've been invited to enjoy this privilege with Jesus.

It is, according to the seventh-century monk and theologian Maximus the Confessor, "a wholly new way of being human."[21]

That sounds like an awful lot (and it is), but that's the outrageous offer from God. It is time to explore some of the traits of this new way of being human. But now, take a step. Just the first one.

It's up to you.

Choose you this day.

FOR PERSONAL REFLECTION

- When was the last time you consciously invited Jesus into your day-to-day life?
- Think of one way you've seen the Spirit of God working in your life this week.

6

CHAIN REACTION

On Thanksgiving, my dad died.

You might think it difficult to give thanks on that day; however, I did so easily. And now, no matter the exact date of that Thursday each year, this holiday will forever intertwine with my thoughts of a godly father, a man who taught his family how to love boldly. Could this be part of what Paul meant to "give thanks in all circumstances?"[1] I was not grateful for the loss, but for the one we lost. At the end, I was also grateful for what death finally brought.

You see, he was no longer in pain.

It sounds strange to admit the odd, awkward relief that flowed alongside the grief. Despite multiple surgeries and interventions on his spine, for years he was in constant and increasing neurological pain. That this pain traced back to an accident involving a drunk driver only added to the injustice of it all.

I never did get to a place of giving thanks for that moment that changed everything for him, nor for the torment he endured.

This comes as no surprise to God, of course. Through the years, we talked about it often. He graciously listened to my unvarnished prayers and questions. Kara Powell and her associates at the Fuller Youth Institute have a saying: "It's not doubt that's toxic to faith. It's silence."[2]

There was no toxic silence.

Our questions were asked and cried and prayed. And though none of us have more than incomplete answers at this point, God responded to my family as he still does, with his presence. We will get a fuller account someday, I believe this. Until then, God is near, and that is enough.

For those who've not experienced this, such words may sound like a neatly tied bow. I assure you, there is more to it. Never denying the present struggle, we never lost sight (for very long) of a future hope. This truth was big enough to live in. It still is. *God is our ever-present help . . .*

Just like he was on that Thanksgiving Day.

THE EDGE OF ETERNITY

Like many families in the closing days of a patriarch, ours gathered to laugh, cry, and tell stories of this man we loved. By the end, it seemed we'd left nothing unsaid to him, though he seemed less and less in our presence. For reasons I could never have orchestrated, at that final hour, it was just me—and then my brother—in the room. The hospice nurses who know better than most told us it would not be long.

Here we stood on that seam where the spiritual overlaps and then overtakes the physical. What could Dad hear? What was he thinking, seeing? He stirred twice but could say nothing. There were only three men in the hospital room that day, but the room seemed fuller still as heaven pushed in close.

It wouldn't be long now.

After all the waiting, the final moments still rushed in with surprise. I began to read Scriptures that spoke of God's faithfulness, the reality of the Resurrection, a hope that does not disappoint. And then those beautiful words of Paul written at the end of his own journey: *I have fought the good fight, run the race . . .* Dad was near the end, and I wanted him to know he'd fought the good fight.

When I could no longer read through watery eyes, I whispered a few things more and kissed his forehead. Chris, my brother, did the same. With his two sons on either side, this tired and noble man's breathing deepened and then slowed.

We were close.

When I was out of Scriptures and almost out of tears, we prayed one more time and then sang his favorite hymn:

> *Blessed assurance, Jesus is mine!*
> *O what a foretaste of glory divine!*
> *Heir of salvation, purchase of God,*
> *Born of his Spirit, washed in his blood.*
>
> *This is my story, this is my song,*
> *Praising my Savior, all the day long;*
> *This is my story, this is my song,*
> *Praising my Savior all the day long.*[3]

When we'd finished, he was gone. By some divine grace, God allowed us to sing our father into his presence.

And now my Dad knows.

He knows of that glory divine. He knows peace. Healing. Relief. He knows the face of Jesus.

But he is beginning to know of something else.

THE LEGACY OF A LIFE

Now my dad knows more fully a legacy that will stretch through countless families.

The nature of his work as a psychologist meant that there were many private and, no doubt, difficult moments when God worked through his expertise. Unfortunately, many of those stories of long-term healing never quite made it back to him. Perhaps now, outside the bounds of time and confidentiality, Jesus is connecting the dots.

He would sometimes wonder aloud if he'd done enough with his life. Often this was the pain talking, but other times, I believe the question was formed out of a heart still susceptible to doubt. It's not an unfamiliar question, is it?

Does the faithful life of one really matter?

Of course it does. He would tell you that. You already know it's true—just like you "know" your multiplication tables. But do you *know that you know* this in the deepest parts of you? Each of us, at certain times, grows susceptible to the nagging nibbles of self-doubt on their way to a self-destructive thought: *What I do isn't going to make that big a difference in the big scheme of things.*

> Does the faithful life of one really matter? Of course it does.

I couldn't disagree with you more.

YOU DON'T HAVE TO BE A HALL OF FAMER

A "hall of fame" denotes a hallowed place where people who are extremely good at what they do are recognized by their peers. Induction into the Baseball Hall of Fame or the Rock & Roll Hall of Fame carries weight. It implies significance, a lasting memory of one's contributions. This life, this career, will not be soon forgotten.

A hall of fame is reserved for the best of the best.

Some people refer to Hebrews 11 as a hall of fame or, as we preachers like to put it, "the Hall of Faith" (see what happened there?). The writer lists several of the great heroes from what we would call the Old Testament. Noah, Sarah, Isaac, Rahab . . . these men and women trusted God at strategic junctures in history, to great effect. They exhibited what the Bible calls faith, trusting what God promised each of them, even when they could only see so far. Choices were made—difficult, costly choices—and God changed the world through their obedience.

Keep reading this extraordinary chapter, and you'll sense the writer running out of room on the page and time on the clock:

> And what more shall I say? I do not have time to tell
> about Gideon, Barak, Samson and Jephthah, about
> David and Samuel and the prophets . . .

And then eventually this:

> There were others.[4]

Others? That's all we get? Who were they? Some I'm sure we could name. But not all. While the big names were making big splashes, there were others quietly doing the right thing. And God did something remarkable with their faith. We don't have their names yet, but God knows.

And now they know . . . how he worked through them, how their legacy stretches through the generations.

I dare not suggest who this author had in mind, but to stir the imagination, let's look at three mostly forgotten heroes whose lives altered history.

Their faithfulness started a chain reaction.

THE WOMAN WHO SAVED CHRISTMAS

Who might be the woman who saved Christmas? Mary? Elizabeth? Mrs. Wise Man, who packed a big lunch for that long journey? No, no, and no. Her name is Jehosheba, and she protected the family line of King David from complete annihilation.

In 2 Samuel 7, God makes specific promises regarding the

descendants of David. Through the house of David and his lineage, God will establish a throne forever. When these kings do wrong (and that happened way too often), there would be stark consequences (and there were). But God's steadfast love would remain.

Over time, this promise took on more details: Eventually, the prophets would look and long for the ultimate descendant of David, the Messiah. This is what the world would need—Israel's promised one, God's King, the son of David.

But there was a moment when that whole line was almost wiped out. The story reads like something a Hollywood screenwriter would dream up—complicated family trees, shocking betrayals, vengeance, and more than a little violence.

Here it is in a nutshell (you can read the full story in 2 Kings 9–11):

It didn't take long for the country to fall apart after David. There was his son (Solomon), and then his son, and then civil war cracked Israel into two separate and rival nations: to the north was Israel—they got the name and the silverware. To the south was Judah—they got the house and the dog. Technically, they kept the capital of Jerusalem and the Temple which resided in it.

Not that it always mattered much.

Early on, the north was ruled by an incredibly evil and pagan pair—King Ahab and Queen Jezebel and their offspring. The south—which was the line of David—had a few good kings but mostly bad ones. In one of those arrangements that history thinks a good idea, a princess of the north (the daughter of Ahab and Jezebel) was married to a king of the south. After a series of betrayals, bloody coups, and vows for revenge, the two houses are committed to wiping the other out.

Things aren't working out at all.

The princess of the north—who has now become the queen mother—starts killing off what's left of the royal family (including her own grandsons) so she alone can rule. It appears the line of King David will come to an end at the hands of this avenging grandma. But one of her own daughters, Jehosheba, snatches an infant boy, her nephew and the heir to the throne, from those being executed.

This was no small act of courage.

Remember, she has just witnessed the cold-blooded extermination of her family by her own mother. And yet she intervenes. For six years, she and her husband, the high priest (and presumably one of the remaining worshipers of God in that vile chaos) hide this little one, until he turns seven. In a heart-pounding turn of events, the young boy, Joash, is revealed at the Temple amid shock and cheers of "Long live the king!" He's crowned, and his crazy grandma is dealt with.

It reads like a screenplay.

It would have been easy for this almost forgotten woman to passively shrug her shoulders. The long story of her family was one of rebellion and idolatry. Her own grandmother, Jezebel, was an evil woman. Her power-thirsty mom was pruning the family tree. What could she do?

But Jehosheba was a woman who worshiped the one true God. Rejecting the lies handed down to her, she chose a different path.

This barely known woman rescued a little boy—and with him, the last hope for the messianic line to continue. Did God need her to keep his plan alive in this bloody chapter of history? Of course not, but looking back, it's very clear he used her courage to preserve the house and lineage of David.

Thanks for saving Christmas, Aunt Jehosheba.

THE NEPHEW WHO SAVED HIS UNCLE (AND HELPED START A REVOLUTION)

The apostle Paul is regularly recognized as one of most important figures in Christianity and one of the most influential people in history. But that influence was almost cut short.

After another trip to plant churches throughout Greece and Turkey, Paul was drawn back to Jerusalem, the epicenter of the Jesus movement. He understood that people there loathed him for preaching about Jesus with such conviction. As a prominent scholar of Judaism, Paul continually showed how Jesus fit perfectly into the oneness of God. No matter how eloquent or airtight his explanations, for some, this still sounded like a betrayal of his Jewish faith. To others, it was simply a threat to their influence over the masses. Either way, Paul's detractors often crossed the line toward violent hatred.

Sure enough, upon his return to the great city, a stewing mob gathered to beat him to death. In an effort to tamp down the riot, Roman guards seize Paul (who's done nothing wrong), wrap him in chains, and drag him inside, where the local military unit was garrisoned. Even as he's led up the stairs into this historic fortress, he tells the crowd one more time about Jesus.

It doesn't go over well. (For you public speakers, any time the crowd shouts that you should die while they are flinging dust in the air,[5] things do not go well.)

After a night in the fortress, he's released to state his case to the religious leaders of the city. Some of the teachers of the law see nothing wrong with Paul's words, but others react so violently that the Roman commander is afraid Paul will be "torn to pieces" by them.[6]

Another night behind bars.

That night, God told him in a vision he would finally get to Rome—the capital of the entire empire. According to his own letter to Roman Christians (written a few years earlier), he longed to go there. And why not? One could not imagine a more strategically influential city in the first century. Preach the gospel here, and who knows where it would reach? What great news—God had said it would now happen.

Except he was going to be ambushed and killed the next day.

Or so thought the forty men who'd vowed they would not eat or drink until the apostle was dead. They would wait until Paul left the barracks the next day to ambush and kill him. A foolproof plan except for this:

> When the son of Paul's sister heard of this plot, he went
> into the barracks and told Paul.[7]

Paul called one of the guards and told him to take this young man (probably a boy, really) to the captain of the guard. The kid told him everything. With the plot now exposed, a detachment of 270 soldiers accompanied Paul up the coast to a city called Caesarea that very night.

And with that, the ambush was ambushed.

Caesarea became a two-year detour mired in a corrupt legal system. Paul must've thought he would never get to Rome. But he did. After a horrible voyage across the sea—the ship's crew almost killing him, a hurricane, a shipwreck, and a poisonous viper latching onto his hand—Paul arrives in the great city.

He is still a prisoner in chains.

But at least he's in Rome.

He showed up in Rome when it was "the most conspicuous spot on the earth . . . the centre of all the movements of the Empire."[8] This was the hub from which the spokes reached to all points of a vast domain.

For the next two years, Paul awaits his trial before Caesar (which likely never came). He is allowed a house which he rented and in which he stayed . . . under arrest, chained to a guard who monitored his every move. To the undiscerning ear, this sounds like defeat: Paul was muzzled and muted.

Except he wasn't. In his letter to the Philippians, he mentions something powerful was happening because of those chains. The gospel was being advanced.

As a result, it has become clear throughout the whole palace guard and to everyone else that I am in chains for Christ.[9]

These privileged Praetorian guard members were entrusted to guard Caesar himself, and as such, they were very closely connected to the seat of power. And it appears some of them are beginning to understand who Jesus is. No wonder this development encouraged the Christians of Rome to "dare all the more to proclaim the gospel without fear."[10]

Here's the picture: a soldier is chained to Paul. He thinks Paul is the prisoner. But Paul sees it another way. He's got a captive audience who is never able to leave the room as Paul teaches the Scriptures to visitors, debates theology, and explains prophecy. They see and hear him dictate letters to churches and people he loves. They watch him pore over the Hebrew Scriptures. No doubt, they hear his passionate prayers.

Little by little over those two years, something advances through that group of elite soldiers.

Now the gospel is working its way through the barracks, but also through families, through friendships and conversation inside Rome itself. No, there was no city-wide revival. Waves of persecution would soon roll through the early church, forging a steely resolve in the Christians of the late first century. And yet, they not only survived but prevailed. According to Rodney Stark, Christianity grew at the rate of *40 percent per decade* during the first several decades.[11]

This number is astounding, and the reasons are myriad—all guided by the sovereign hand of the one who first said "Go." Is it too much to suggest that one of those factors involved Christianity's most ardent apologist living under the emperor's nose for two years? Look at a glossed-over comment at the end of Philippians, and sense just how close to Caesar the gospel was thriving: "All God's people here send you greetings, *especially those who belong to Caesar's household."* [12]

Were these slaves in service to the Emperor's palace? Could this refer to some in his own family? We don't know. But because of Paul's presence in Rome, the story of Jesus had broken free in the royal palace.

From Rome, he wrote the letters of Ephesians, Philippians, Colossians, and Philemon, exhorting believers for two thousand years and counting. From Rome, he invited the soldiers of the Praetorian guard—many of whom would eventually retire in the provinces—to follow Jesus. From Rome, the famous roads radiating out from the city would now carry others. "Mostly these nameless Christians were merchants, slaves, and others who traveled for various reasons, but whose travel provided the opportunity for the expansion of the Christian message." [13]

The revolution of grace was alive and well in the center of the empire, and her roads and ships would now carry the message. Is it fair to say at least part of that revolution reaches back to a young nephew who saved his uncle?

I say yes.

He started a chain reaction.

NUCLEAR FISSION FOR DUMMIES (LIKE ME)

Scientists in the twentieth century found that if you bombard the nucleus of certain uranium atom[14] with a neutron, it will split into two or more parts, releasing massive amounts of energy in the process. This also spits out more neutrons that hit and then split other nuclei, and the process of splitting and spitting happens again and again (and again).

This is what scientists call a chain reaction.

Just one little atomic action starts a reaction that releases more power and energy than you can imagine. And that's the point: One little particle strategically aimed has that big an effect.

Think of what happens if one person—in the right place at the right time—does the right thing. They may not be famous or powerful. But that which is released by one act of obedience dwarfs anything a physics professor can describe.

Jesus speaks at one point of the inherent power of the Holy Spirit at work in us.[15] In the New Testament the Greek word is *dynamis*—a dynamic, dare I say, *explosive* power. It is not ours to manufacture or manipulate, for "this all-surpassing power is from God and not from us."[16]

We underestimate the power involved when taking that first small, even unnoticed step. We forget how God will use that obedience to ripple through lives that affect other lives. We simply will not understand this side of heaven the magnitude of this powerful good released. Its effect will echo long after we're gone.

Sometimes the chain reaction starts with a simple invitation.

THE LITTLE BROTHER WHO MADE A BIG DIFFERENCE

In the Gospels, we see Jesus gathering an inner circle of students. And while we might politely assert that eleven of these disciples qualify for the hall of fame, most have difficulty naming the whole bunch. To be fair, some are barely mentioned (James son of Alphaeus, anyone?).

When we think of potential hall of famers, we usually think of Peter, James, and John, with Peter (the nickname Jesus gave Simon) being the most famous of all. You might recall who told this future leader of the early church about Jesus.

His little brother.

Andrew, like his brother Simon, was initially a fisherman on the Sea of Galilee. But Andrew and his friend John (the Gospel writer) were also followers of the famous and very loud prophet we call John the Baptist. In those days, he was the one telling people to get ready, for God's Messiah was about to step onto the scene. John the Baptist and Jesus knew each other (being cousins and all, not to mention that baptism). One day, he pointed out Jesus to those two disciples of his and proclaimed, "Look, the Lamb of God!"[17]

That's quite a statement, and those two disciples were intrigued.

Andrew and John follow Jesus, who soon invites them to spend the day with him. That's all it took—Andrew was convinced. What does he do next?

> The first thing Andrew did was to find his brother
> Simon and tell him, "We have found the Messiah" (that
> is, the Christ). And he brought him to Jesus.[18]

You know the rest of the story. Simon Peter, after a tumultuous start, is forever changed and commissioned by the resurrected Jesus. He becomes the de facto leader of the early church, preaching his first sermon in Jerusalem, after which three thousand people were baptized. Many would suggest this itself set off a chain reaction that became the Christian movement. But now you know the full story: It really started when Peter's little brother invited him to meet Jesus.

IT'S CALLED FAITH FOR A REASON

Some chain reactions take longer than we want. I've already admitted as much. Even in the stories just mentioned, it often took (gulp) years for those involved to see how God was working through their faithfulness. And in none of those stories did they fully grasp how far the effect of that one step would reach.

If you've ever allowed yourself to

> By all means, dream big, for God is even bigger. Then take the next small step in front of you. And the one after that.

dream of making a big difference in this world, you can. You will. But here's how: Stay faithful and focused on the next step. By all means, dream big, for God is even bigger. Then take the next small step in front of you. And the one after that. For all the talk of vision, you and I will never see as far down the road as we'd like.

This is where faith comes in.

When the Bible speaks of faith, it's not a feeling or a hunch. It's a confidence, a conviction of something still to come. The faith described in Hebrews 11 has an eye toward the future. In fact, this is so pointed toward the future that what we read as *faith* is getting very close to another word we will soon consider: *hope*.

That's why these hall of famers made the choices they did. It's why all the unnamed others did the right thing, the hard thing, the unnoticed thing.

They believed God had already done great things—they'd already experienced his great love and power. But then this—they believed he wasn't finished doing great things. This is how you trust what God will do in the future when you're still in the middle of the story. Remember what he's already done for you, and from this, the confidence grows. No wonder this pivotal chapter begins with these memorable words: "Faith is confidence in what we hope for and assurance about what we do not see."[19]

When the Bible speaks of faith, it's not a feeling or a hunch.

There it is again—*assurance*.

This is how my Dad and all the "others" lived their significant lives—with a blessed assurance. Even when you cannot see enough. Even when you wonder how much your individual life matters, as so many of these hall of famers did at various points. You return again and again to that assurance of what you cannot yet see. This is how you take the next faithful step and the next one after that.

You are assured that there is more. That he is more.

Now my dad and countless others know what it is for which they hoped. Now they see the grand work of our sovereign God and how the choices and fragments of their faith fit together for his glory.

Until that day comes for you and me—we know enough.

Remember what God has already done. Turn toward the future, where he waits. Now trust that he'll meet you there. He'll meet you in that very next step. He'll help you take it—that's how much you need him. But on the seam of what was and what will be, remember God is still up to something. This is how chain reactions start. This is how the world can change again.

This is our story.

This is our song.[20]

FOR PERSONAL REFLECTION

- Do you believe that God wants to use you to impact the Kingdom? Why or why not?
- What is one lesson from this chapter that you will apply this week?

RUN TO THE BORDER

"I'LL TAKE QUIRKY AMERICAN HISTORY for $500, Alex."

The answer is: It took place around the Tug Fork River during the years following the American Civil War. (Nothing?) Try this: Devil Anse and Rand'l were major characters. Or this: Kidnapping, death, and downright destruction peppered this valley for decades. (Still nothing?) One more try: It was Devil Anse Hatfield and Rand'l McCoy. Ah, of course, now you've got it.

"What is: the infamous feud between the Hatfields and McCoys."

The rumbles of this hostility started in the Civil War, but many trace this feud back to a pig that was stolen—or not, depending on whom you ask. There was a trial, a witness, and a verdict. And then someone died. This conflict kept recycling over a variety of issues . . . moonshine, affairs, land disputes, and vendettas all fueled by a festering hate that bled into the Tug River valley. Theoretically it ended in 1891, but it wasn't until 1976 that the families shook hands. Still, a legal battle erupted over a family cemetery in 2000. Finally, in 2003 descendants from both sides signed a contract—on a morning news show, no less—in an attempt to inspire a post-9/11 nation to unity.[1]

It all sounds made-up and all too real. Not always the bloodshed, but the lingering bad blood that flows between peoples and political parties, between neighborhoods and churches, and yes, families. How much of our world resembles those battling clans?

That is not the way God intended us to live.

Human existence was not originally designed for feuds and vendettas. Though we may easily drift into such patterns with the help of our fallenness and the spiritual forces conspiring against us, buried deep is an aching notion. Time is being wasted. Life is being sucked from our all-too-fleeting days on earth. We can feel it in our bones. We may not always do better, but in our heart of hearts, we know better. We want better.

WHAT WE REALLY WANT

Scott Sauls sums it up nicely: "The sheer popularity of self-help books points to the reality that humans live with an insatiable longing for something more, something better."[2] With continued apologies to your Aunt Ethel after mentioning her in chapter 2, we don't need another self-help book. Yet there is a lingering sense that we've missed the life that is still available. Scott continues: "Our innate, unshakable longing to be better suggests that deep down, we don't really believe that to err is human after all."[3]

We know we were made for more.

So we pray, we read our Bibles, we confess, we tell God we want more out of this life, that we want to grow and make progress and sense that we are on our way out of these doldrums of the mediocre.

We want to *flourish*.

Of course, this term now used across many disciplines can easily become the next word-of-the-month from overuse. And yet there is much here that others, from Andy Crouch in his book *Strong and Weak* to the writings of theologian Jonathan Pennington and others have grounded in biblical wisdom.

> The righteous will flourish like a palm tree,
>> they will grow like a cedar of Lebanon;
>> planted in the house of the LORD,
>> they will flourish in the courts of our God.[4]

The notion of flourishing implies the ongoing process of growth we see in all things living. This is the natural and God-given way of life. Like a blade of grass pushing through the smallest crack in the sidewalk, we want more. Life seeks what it needs to exist fully.

This is not the lusty "more" of narcissism—wanting more for more's sake. It is certainly not the greedy *more* of material prosperity couched in Christianly terms. It is a soulish hunger. We expect more from ourselves and the world in which we live. More of life in all its fullness and richness. More justice and love. More depth to our relationships and purpose to our work. More satisfaction and challenge and rest.

Hugh Whelchel correctly notes that "in the Old Testament, the concept of flourishing is best described by the Jewish word *shalom*."[5] You've come across this word on these pages and many others, I'm sure. In recent years, scholars have correctly stretched our understanding well beyond the idea of peace. It is more than peace, more than a lack of conflict. Shalom is a put-togetherness. A wholeness. A this-is-how-things-were-meant-to-be rightness.

> Shalom is a put-togetherness. A wholeness. A this-is-how-things-were-meant-to-be rightness.

This is the way we were meant to live—in "right relationship with God, with others, and with God's good creation."[6]

A WAY OF BEING IN THE WORLD

It is also the extraordinary invitation offered on a hillside in Galilee two thousand years ago. In the most sublime sermon ever preached, Jesus describes the difference-making life in all its hot and coldness—nothing lukewarm here. And he begins it all with nine statements we commonly call "the Beatitudes" from the Latin *beātus*, meaning "happy" or "blessed." This is how translators usually render the Greek word, *makarios*, which kicks off each of these statements. Pennington makes a strong case that a word like "happy" or "blessed" barely plumbs the depths of what Jesus is saying, however. He writes: "Jesus begins his public ministry by painting a picture of what the state of true God-centered human flourishing looks like."[7]

This is the larger-than, fuller-than, more-than life with God in charge right now, even as we trust him to make things right someday. And it is Jesus, our Savior and Sage who shows us the way. He is inviting those on the hillside (and the rest of us) into a "way of being in the world."[8]

Like an instrument in perfect tune, a profound sense of well-being resonates inside this life. It may seem odd or upside down to the rest of the world, but this is life turned right-side up. No mechanical formulas here, no religious checkpoints, just Jesus painting a stunning image of the fully-alive human experience as image-bearers of the Most High God. And tucked into that glorious opening come these timely words: "Blessed are the peacemakers, for they shall be called the children of God."[9]

The flourishing life that satisfies us in the present and hints of what is yet to come must involve peacemaking. Is this speaking of large-scale peacemaking? Small, private work? There is room and need for both in our Hatfield-and-McCoy world.

Notice it doesn't say peacekeepers who avoid the uncomfortable. Nor does it say peacefakers who won't stand up for truth. No, this is a very active concept. These are the people who end hostilities and even bring the quarrelsome together. It is the absence of conflict, but so much more.

It is shalom.

A FAMILY RESEMBLANCE

When you champion peace, work for peace, make peace, when you are a broker of shalom, Jesus says you'll be called a child of God. For those sensitized to anything that hints at working your way into God's Kingdom: Peacemaking does not earn your forgiveness. This is not a behavioral key that unlocks your entrance to the Kingdom.

Our story will always be anchored in the grace of our Lord Jesus and the price he paid on the cross. Still, we cannot ignore his words here. Peacemaking is such a hallmark characteristic of God being in charge that Jesus singles it out as a family trait. Leon Morris says it as such: "There is something godlike in bringing peace to people and people to peace."[10]

In a world that can barely imagine peace, when we enter the fray as peacemakers, Jesus says, we bear a family resemblance.

Dr. Pennington rightly points us to Eugene Peterson's words about how the Bible instructs readers overall as a helpful way to apply these Beatitudes:

> [Scripture] does not present us with a moral code and tell us "Live up to this"... The biblical way is to tell a story and in the telling invite: "Live *into* this— this is what it looks like to be human in this God-made and God-ruled world; this is what is involved in becoming and maturing as a human being."[11]

> Peacemaking is such a hallmark characteristic of God being in charge that Jesus singles it out as a family trait.

Let's see if, for the remainder of this chapter, we might discover a way to "live into" the beauty and power of peacemaking. To do so, let's narrow the scope to one aspect of this practice. Both shocking and soothing, neither easy nor natural to most, this one act could prevent significant damage being inflicted by our feuding selves on ourselves.

For better or worse, this is something you can start doing almost immediately, for the opportunity will soon be upon you.

ANOTHER LESSON FROM HISTORY

It is the time after the Exodus, God's massive rescue of his people from four centuries of slavery. A fledgling nation is now out of Egypt and making her way back to the land of her ancestors—Abraham, Isaac, and Jacob. A land God had promised to them hundreds of years earlier. On first glance, the fortified cities dotting the landscape of Canaan intimidated the children of Israel. As you'll recall, they turned on Moses and (more importantly) the mighty Yahweh, who had promised to protect them. Only Joshua and Caleb trusted God in that moment. And only they remained after forty wilderness-wandering years. Their disobedient peers were now all but gone.

Israel stands again on the edge of her future.

The conquests of the land fill the book of Joshua. The one-time spy and protégé of Moses is now his successor. It is he who leads the people across the Jordan River as God makes a way into this Land of Promise. And yes, this brings up the sorts of questions some aren't sure they can ask in a faith community. Ask them. Move into the topic with a humble mind and soft heart. God will meet you there.

This isn't the book, nor am I likely the author to take you through all that such a discussion entails. For our purposes, allow me this brief summary.

A DIFFICULT SUBJECT BARELY EXPLAINED

These are difficult chapters to fully explain, as God gives specific instructions on how to deal with the Canaanite culture. Its culture and the religions on which it existed were enormously dehumanizing. Elsewhere in the Old Testament (Leviticus 18, to be exact), some of these dark and destructive practices are listed. Cultic prostitution and the abuse of young women was a part of their so-called worship. So, too, was human sacrifice. In this brutally primitive time, God decreed this must stop. Such practices will not be folded into the worldview of the Israelites, and this will NOT be how they worship Yahweh.[12]

Difficult subject, yes. And this cursory explanation only stirs up more questions. Go further. Ask more. Stay open to all of the story. You will find yourself, at times, even more unsettled. But also this: When Abraham himself in an early story asked God if he would essentially go "too far" in his judgment of Sodom and Gomorrah, God seems to have assured him (and the rest of us) with an insight. Abraham asks humbly—"Will not the Judge of all the earth do right?"[13]

Not a simple answer, but I hang on to the character of God when the honest stories of Scripture unsettle me.

God was revealing his plan, entering history, making a way. And protecting the story along the way. Again, remember to look for the whole story. At times God also brought judgment against the people of Israel as they wandered from his love and guidance. If it helps to think of it this way, God didn't play favorites in the Old Testament. He's always wanting and working to restore and make things right with anyone who turns to him. Anyone. God longed for humanity to finally and ultimately trust that he just might have their best interests at heart.

This has never changed.

Now, back to our history lesson. It is years later. The land has been mostly conquered, though not fully "settled." It is another time of transition. Joshua is now an old man. The twelve tribes of Israel will now be allotted their portion of the land. It's all been agreed upon. Maps drawn. Stakes claimed. The wars are over.

Finally, it is time to go home.

A PROMISE KEPT

But first, the weathered and wise general summons two-and-a-half tribes to Shiloh, where the Tabernacle was located, for a special send-off. He brought them there to express gratitude for their service and for keeping a promise.

A couple more details here will help. The tribes of Reuben and Gad (and half of the large tribe of Manasseh) saw land on the east side of the Jordan that looked good for them and their flocks before they ever crossed into Canaan. Years ago, before any conflict, they asked Moses if they could stake out something to the east.

"Yes," was his answer, as long as they helped clear out the ugliness on the west side of the river. Here they are, seven years later, and Joshua is commending them for keeping their word. In his farewell address, he also exhorts them to not forget their identity nor the one true God who redeemed them: "Love the Lord your God. Obey Him. Hold fast to Him. You'll be farther away from us, but never forget to whom you belong."[14]

Then he blesses them and sends them home.

What a journey that must've been.

A SERIOUS MISSTEP

Imagine that grateful trip home: sharing stories of valor, shedding tears of grief. Before long they approach the iconic natural boundary of the Jordan River. Years earlier God had done a mighty thing here when the river was at flood stage, all to make a way for the nation to cross over. More memories. More gratitude. They are likely not far from Jericho. Who could forget that miraculous victory? With full hearts, if not clear heads, someone gets an idea before they cross the river, and they stumble:

> When they came to Geliloth near the Jordan in the land of Canaan, the Reubenites, the Gadites and the half-tribe of Manasseh built an imposing altar there by the Jordan.[15]

This imposing altar was so huge, you could see it from a distance, apparently. It resembled the altar in the Tabernacle back at Shiloh. In other words, it looked like the kind of place where you'd offer sacrifices. It appeared to everyone else these two-and-a-half tribes were already starting their own religion.

And with that, the rest of Israel was ready to rumble.

> When the Israelites heard that they had built the altar . . . the whole assembly of Israel gathered at Shiloh to go to war against them.[16]

That fell apart quickly, don't you think? At first glance, the story seems so removed from our times. And yet, it isn't. To live into the life of peacemaking, we must learn from the traps tucked in this strange chapter from Israel's early history.

ANATOMY OF AN (ALMOST) EPIC FAIL

Let's look at a few elements of a near disaster that also find their way into our current interactions with each other.

Mistakes will happen. Looking back, we see that construction of this monument was unwise. Though we'll soon find out these eastbound tribe members' hearts were innocent of any idolatry, it still gave the appearance of what they'd fought so hard to reject. In an emotionally charged environment, even small miscues have the potential to ignite large conflicts. Do not be shocked by the imperfect ways of others. When they happen, these are the moments to work for peace.

Hearsay isn't worth warring over. "When the Israelites heard . . .": These dangerous words often serve as the tipping point on which peace is made or lost, *when you hear something* that someone else has said or done. In our day, this would also include the virulent strains of a social-media rumor, but often it still takes the age-old form of someone "informing" you of a potential offense. Hearsay alone—even if it is partially accurate—rarely offers you the benefit of context. Don't go to war over someone else's version of what happened.

"The worst" becomes the default assumption. This truth is why hearsay alone will get you in trouble. The nine-and-a-half tribes were immediately convinced the two-and-a-half tribes had built this altar "in rebellion." Are we any different when we first hear of some unfriendly development? Some will try to suggest they are realists and thus not easily duped. More likely, it is our default reaction toward the worst—we have come to expect (and even want?) such things to be true.

> Hearsay isn't worth warring over.

This is a conditioned response for many in a world where the sensationally ugly is foisted on us daily. Through cues we no longer even notice and the juicy reward of feeling superior, we have settled into the habit of looking for the most horrible explanation of any situation. Resist this at every turn.

People grow accustomed to conflict. For seven long years, these people had battled against darkness. The casualties of war were significant, but without giving it much thought, they were immediately ready to spill more blood. Stay in the conflict long enough, and somewhere along the way you start thinking it's normal, or at least unavoidable. Is it possible that in our own fractious times we, too, have grown accustomed to warring? Think back on the histories of your own relationships with others and other organizations—does it always end the same? Have we forgotten how to speak without battle-axes and battering rams?

In seemingly short order, young Israel is about to destroy itself from the inside, a phenomenon with which we are all too familiar. There must be a better way. Our insides scream for a better way. Is there something within this story that offers concrete clues of shalom-building? Can we find in this volatile chapter any hints of how we might live into this life of peacemaking?

MAKING PEACE BEFORE THE WAR STARTS

What follows is the choice to move toward peace when so much hangs in the balance. Actually, it is a series of choices that set off a series of reactions. Let's slow down the narrative to extract a few of those pivotal decisions.

Passion for what is right is not wrong. With the army on full alert, someone thought to send a delegation to the tribes on the border. Heading that group was Phineas, the high priest. He was known for being anything but lukewarm. *Zealous* is the word used to describe him when he stood against evil at a horrible juncture in Israel's recent past.[17] He does not want Israel corrupted. It's almost impossible to overstate this danger and how throughout the coming years, this nation would be seduced by these dark and destructive practices. It was their biggest downfall, polluting the very land God gave them.

Here, Phineas lives for the honor of God—and what a powerful need we have for such men and women. But is it possible that in our zeal, we focus less and less on the ways of God? Do we settle for being zealous about merely being right? For winning the debate? Even worse, for making someone pay? When did any of this make its way into our job descriptions? It is noticeably absent in Jesus' description of the flourishing life. It is also absent in Phineas. This zealous man could've taken everyone over the cliff—all while invoking his "rightness" and commitment to God.

But he didn't.

Ask curious and humble questions. This is an integral step that must not be overlooked. Phineas and the delegation wanted their facts straight before blood was shed. The question is pointed, but rings of godly sorrow: "How could you break faith with the God of Israel like this?"[18]

To wait for the answer after asking such a question requires a humble posture of the heart. Proverbs 18:13 warns that "to answer before listening—that is folly and shame." Even when God's people think they've got it all figured out, there is an underlying humility: *What if I was wrong about them? What if there was more to the story? What if I stay open to their answer?* What heartache is spared when we slow down enough to allow those initial assumptions to be corrected or at least clarified. Be the one who asks the questions with a willingness to hear the answers.

The problem was stated out loud. There is an expression in English about acknowledging "the elephant in the room." At this point, the delegation does just that. They remind their fellow Israelites of a very bad (and recent) memory when men from Israel were literally seduced into the darkness mentioned earlier. God took shockingly decisive action—a plague on the whole community. It is still fresh in their minds: "'If you rebel against the LORD today, tomorrow he will be angry with the whole community of Israel.'"[19]

> Be the one who asks the questions with a willingness to hear the answers.

"Please don't go down this road—it will end in disaster for all of us." They were specific and honest about their concerns and fears. There would be consequences for all involved. Had the eastern tribes counted the cost of this mistake? Long before Paul penned his letter to the Ephesians, these Israelites spoke "the truth in love."[20] Do we love someone enough to speak truth without destroying them or the hope of future relationship?

A way back to relationship was offered, even if it was costly. The nine-and-a-half plead: "If your land (on the other side of the Jordan) is defiled, stay on our side of the river. If things have changed, and it doesn't feel safe or right, *share the land with us.*"[21] If you now think that land is outside the blessing of God, we'll make room." What an astounding offer. When was the last time you said that to someone with whom you're about to go to war? "I'll make things right, even if it costs me."

This is where we most bear a likeness to our Savior.

I remember being a part of an important conversation about racial reconciliation. I say I was "a part" of it. Mostly I was listening, lamenting, confessing, and then listening some more. At one point, I noted how daunting the task of bridging significant gaps seemed to me and how long others in the room had pursued peace at great cost to themselves. I must've given the impression these costs were intimidating me (they were). An older African American woman then graced me with such kind and knowing eyes I could barely stand the power of her gaze. "If you're going to be about building bridges, remember this: Bridges get walked on." There was not a hint of the faux martyrdom that creeps into my voice at times. This was sheer courage laced with grace.

It was also one of the most Christ-like things I've ever been taught.

"What can I do to make things right for you?" Who asks that question when we know it will cost us something? Yet this is godly love. This is the way to peace. This is the way of Jesus.

They responded with transparency. The two-and-a-half tribes reply: "God knows our hearts on this! Let everyone else know! If our motives were rebellion or disobedience, don't spare us."[22]

(They actually agree with the severity of worshiping outside of God's way.)

But then this: "We wanted it [the altar] to be a witness between us and you and the generations that follow."[23] The thing behind the thing is the eastern tribes are already missing the rest of them. Settling that far to the east worries them. Perhaps they'll soon be forgotten and unwelcome when they come back to worship.

In the middle of a conflict, we tend to only show our supposed strength. Feeling under attack, we "bow up," as my Texas relatives would say. But here, in a moment of disarming honesty, the people admit to feeling a little insecure about moving.

Joshua might've been worried about their isolation leading to a spiritual drift away from God, but they were worried their isolation might lead to a relational drift from their brothers and sisters. "You might reject us in coming generations and forget we were a part of God's plan, that we helped you and that we love the same God."

"So we built this replica—though we'd never do anything with it. It's just a reminder for both of us that we worship the same God."[24]

Phineas saw it from another perspective. When Phineas heard this had nothing remotely to do with idol worship, he was pleased, along with the rest of the delegation. And the tense moment was over. It might not have been the smartest idea, but it was an honest explanation. In essence, Phineas says, "I believe you." No lectures. No "I'm holding this over you." It was over. Are we openhearted enough to believe another explanation, or have we dug in so deep that now it's more about being "right" than being at peace?

He led others to reconciliation. The high priest turned back to the west and reported to the Israelites.[25] Phineas then represented the two-and-a-half when speaking to the nine-and-a-half. Mark it well: As a peacemaker, there will be times when you need to turn back to your own tribe and speak healing truth as only you can. These are heady times, when an army gathers around you, ready for war. When there is a chance for peace, you may be the only one who can speak for the other side. You will be the one who takes the lead. The one who declares "enough is enough."

When the people heard this report, they were glad . . . and praised God. Why? Because they didn't want to spill blood. They didn't want merely to be right. They wanted peace. Are we pleased or are we disappointed in such moments? Beware the adrenaline-laced letdown. When you've assembled the team and ramped up your emotions, it can feel like there's nowhere to go when the conflict is averted. That's one of the reasons they worshiped. I believe they cheered, cried, and thanked God, for this is what they longed for deep down. "And they talked no more about going to war."[26]

We are not accustomed to such outcomes, but they do happen. They can happen. They should happen more often. The flourishing life we were made to live involves making peace. And there will soon be times when such a situation presents itself. Things will escalate quickly. Accusations will fly. Armies will assemble.

It will then be your turn to lead others to peace.

POSTSCRIPT

For a time, this imposing monument at the edge of an almost-disaster had a name: "A Witness Between Us—that the LORD is God."[27] It became a symbol of unity and the God who united them.

All these years later, we have an even greater symbol of our unity. It's more than a monument lost to antiquity. It is the marker standing at the center of it all. This was how God reconciled us to himself. This is how the walls of hostility are still being torn down. The cross of Jesus stands tall in the flourishing life, and we are being invited to live into all that it means and offers.

In light of all he has done and invited us into—today, next week, next month, before the blood starts spilling in our Hatfield-and-McCoy world, before hearts are broken and words are shouted or posted, before friendships are destroyed and bridges dismantled—think back to our little three-thousand-year-old history lesson and try this:

For the sake of peace, for the sake of a flourishing, fully-alive way of being, for the sake of a world that desperately needs a hint of how things could be and will be . . .

Run to the border.

FOR PERSONAL REFLECTION

- How good of a listener are you?
- In what relationship do you long for God's peace and healing?

ANTIFRAGILE . . . SORT OF

I WAS RIDING IN THE BACK of a jeep weaving through the streets of Monrovia next to a giant of a man who, standing tall, was still several inches shorter than me. When I say "a giant," I mean in the sense that you know when you're in the presence of such faith that your own seems small. We were riding and bumping our way through the still-scarred streets of the city. Civil war has left its mark on Liberia in more ways than one—gutted buildings, an entire generation hobbled by the brutality, and a people who've seen more than their share of heartache in the last few decades.

And then the Ebola crisis.

As the death toll mounted during the peak of the Ebola outbreak, there were many factors working against those trying to stop the spread of that horrific disease, the lack of clean water and basic hygiene practices among them. The country director of

Liberia, Austin Nyaplue, told me of his decision to stay as part of a team with Living Water International and keep working. He calmly spoke of soldiers surrounding his team as they dug new boreholes in desperate regions, all while wearing hazmat suits and praying the mysterious virus would not reach them. He spoke of the dramatic drop of the outbreak in areas with clean water and basic sanitation strategies.[1]

Nothing lukewarm here.

I was in that jeep returning to a village I'd visited a decade ago, wondering how things might've changed since then. But mostly, I marveled at the people I continued to encounter who have trusted God in the face of "many dangers, toils, and snares."[2] And still, they believe. They have survived. No, they have prevailed. I see it in quiet smiles and in eyes that have seen the whole eye chart.

My return to Liberia led me to thoughts about my own approach to the uncertainty of this life. As we've now admitted, it is not so clear cut, our path in this world. Jesus has called us into this world and warned of trouble. Our steps along the way may be small, but sometimes they're downright difficult. This journey into the hot and cold flourishing life is no easy trek.

So let me ask the question: How resilient are we?

Please do not see this as a careless rebuttal of the entire human race slowing the spread of a virus. The retreats of which I speak are not wise precautions during a crisis, but foolhardy attempts to avoid discomfort. Do we make the avoidance of struggle our top priority? Do we expect God to make it his? When the trouble Jesus predicted in this world shows up on our doorstep, do we strike out at others (or God)? Do we melt into self-destructing blobs of what we used to be?

How resilient are we?

There is a better way.

BOUNCING BACK?

> *We are afflicted in every way, but not crushed; perplexed, but not driven to despair; persecuted, but not forsaken; struck down, but not destroyed . . .*
>
> 2 CORINTHIANS 4:8-9, ESV

Can you even imagine such a response? Let's try it again: How resilient are you?

Such an interesting word—*resilient*. It conjures up images of someone who survives, yes, but more. The origin of the word traces back to the Latin verb *resilire*, meaning "to leap or spring back."[3] So it's someone who bounces back. In physics, it refers to a material that can absorb the energy of a blow and then release that energy as it "springs back to its original shape."[4]

Who couldn't do with a little more of that in this disruptive and uncertain world? To be able to bounce back from adversity is a good thing. To be able to somehow release the energy of the blow that just landed so you spring back to who you were.

As amazing as that sounds, Paul is describing even more.

What if—and we are about to wade into some radically powerful Scriptures—we could move even beyond being resilient to becoming something more than we were before that storm . . . that loss . . . that injustice . . . that failure . . . that illness?

AN ALMOST FAMILIAR THOUGHT

Bestselling author Nassim Taleb grew up in Lebanon during its own civil war. Educated at Wharton and the University of Paris, he spent over twenty years as a derivatives trader analyzing risks and probable outcomes. (This already puts his thinking a notch—or twelve—above mine on many things.) He then became a researcher and author on the topics of probability and uncertainty and how we handle unpredictable events. In a flurry of thought-provoking and rather blunt (some would say abrasive) observations, peppered with intriguing examples, he offers a thought that sounds *almost* familiar to me.

In his book *Antifragile: Things that Gain from Disorder*, he makes a distinction between three categories:

Fragile   Resilient   Antifragile

We can guess what fragile means. We've just covered what resilient means. What about that third word of his own making? In the prologue, Taleb describes how some structures, systems, and people respond to stress by not cracking or even bouncing back. They improve, growing stronger, wiser. This he sees as the opposite of fragile. "Let us call it antifragile."[5]

Antifragile is not mere resilience (which is at least better than fragile). It is more than snapping back to what was before. "Antifragility is beyond resilience. . . . The resilient resists shocks and stays the same; the antifragile gets better."[6]

Now we're talking.

"Fragile" is how he describes people and organizations whose goal is to minimize all stress and flatten out potential risk and tension. We know how that turns out—you can't live in a hermetically sealed bubble that protects you from trouble. Such attempts to avoid all stress actually make you more fragile.

Thus, a part of his antifragile thesis is to not fear or avoid stress because we can indeed grow stronger in response to it. An obvious example would be how the body responds to exercise—a form of stress—by getting stronger. Not invincible, but stronger. Fair enough. Most of us can point back to some change or shock to our system that left us, in the aftermath, stronger. Wiser. Better. These are often the moments when a great idea shows up—*because it must show up*. Or, as Taleb so memorably puts it, "difficulty is what wakes up the genius."[7]

I like that too.

Much of this makes sense with one little (okay, not so little) caveat.[8] Moving beyond mere resilience into a stronger and wiser existence because of stress sounds *almost familiar* to those who follow Jesus. Don't we encounter such thinking in the New Testament?

MAKING PROGRESS

James wrote this in his letter to Christ followers:

> Consider it pure joy, my brothers and sisters, whenever you face trials of many kinds, because you know that the testing of your faith produces perseverance. Let perseverance finish its work so that you may be mature and complete, not lacking anything.[9]

Paul put it like this to the Christians in Rome:

> We also exult in our tribulations, knowing that tribulation brings about perseverance; and perseverance, proven character; and proven character, hope; and hope does not disappoint, because the love of God has been poured out within our hearts through the Holy Spirit who was given to us.[10]

In both instances, a progression of growth emerges. Truly, this is not merely returning to the status quo, snapping back to the way things were before the storm. No, because of that difficulty I turn to the one who has overcome the world. My faith is maturing. My hope is deepening.

At first glance, verses like these sound nonchalant, almost flippant. "Consider it joy." "Exult in our tribulations." Since we know the context of these letters, we know otherwise. These writers did not take their tribulations lightly. James died for his faith around AD 62. Tradition says he was thrown off the temple heights and beaten with a club for proclaiming Jesus as Messiah. Paul was executed, likely beheaded, outside of Rome in the mid-60s AD.

That doesn't sound nonchalant.

Somehow, in the face of real threats, they had a different perspective on their troubles. They discovered something in those hardest of moments. Not that anyone signs up for these trials or seeks them out. When Paul writes of delighting in weaknesses, insults, hardships, persecutions, and difficulties, this is not a man bent on self-destruction. This is a reaction born out of an observation he then shares: "When I am weak, then I am strong."[11]

It is the power of Christ that rests on him, his grace being enough in the weaker moments.

WHERE STRENGTH LIES

I barely, on my best days, can attest to knowing of what he speaks. But when I can take this longer view of my life and its occasional storms, *I am different*: my faith seems a little more grown up, my hope deeper than it was, my resolve firmer than before.

That's what sounds *almost* familiar to me from Taleb's writing. Almost. The primary difference here is any antifragility that shows up in my life will entail a spiritual component. It will involve more than a mathematical probability around which I've arranged my life. Yes, I need to take responsibility for me. It is so helpful if I shift toward a mindset of developing strength from distress. But neither Paul nor James would ever suggest that you can do this on your own.

To the contrary.

Go back to the opening Scripture and its resounding victory: "afflicted in every way, but not crushed . . . struck down, but not destroyed." And now back one more sentence. "But we have this treasure in jars of clay, to show that the surpassing power belongs to God and not to us."[12] This hope, this power, this light, this life, this treasure is in jars of clay—I'm not sure you can get more fragile than that. This is Paul's point: It's to show the surpassing power belongs to God and not to us.

THAT sounds familiar. There is a different way to live that grows in the middle of the storm, a faith that matures, a hope that deepens. And it will always all come back to the one who has rescued us. Across the pages of Scripture, it's him. Always him. Reaching back to a previous concept, Pennington rightly surmises:

> The Bible, across its whole Christian canon of both Old and New Testaments, is providing its own God-of-Israel-revealed-in-Jesus-Christ answer to the foundational human question of how to flourish and thrive.[13]

It is Jesus who sustains me in the middle of the struggle and pours meaning into the hurt later. This is how endurance begets character, which begets hope—a hope that does not disappoint.

AN UNCOMFORTABLE WORD

It is one thing to map out how such an approach to life makes sense. What happens when the unwanted shows up? It is time to hear from another prominent character of the Gospels and early church.

Only two of Peter's letters find their way into our Bibles, though they pack quite a punch. The first of these was more than likely written from Rome, where he spent the last decade of his life.[14] Eventually he, too, will be executed for his faith.

> It is Jesus who sustains me in the middle of the struggle and pours meaning into the hurt later.

The Peter we encounter here is different from the brash man of the Gospels. You might recall that he had the gall to correct Jesus from time to time (which, for the record, never works out). He even tried to convince Jesus to skip the cross—out of misguided love and a strong sense of self-preservation.[15]

This Peter is different. Now he speaks of facing the suffering head-on. The verb *suffer* is used a dozen times in 1 Peter. With eyes wide open, he sees more of reality than before. Now he wants the same for his readers. Horribly tough times are coming, but believers need not be defeated.

Such heartening words. Yet, the one word on which much of these are built shows up late in Peter's letter. It is not our favorite word in any form. It clangs on my own tin ears, especially as a verb:

Humble yourselves, therefore, under God's mighty hand,
that he may lift you up in due time.[16]

Did you catch it? *Humble* yourselves.

This becomes an essential part of how we face the roughest edges of life. The surpassing power to thrive belongs to God, not me. In the previous verse, Peter has just quoted the same proverb[17] James does[18] in reminding us that "God opposes the proud but shows favor to the humble."[19]

> *Humble* yourselves. This becomes an essential part of how we face the roughest edges of life.

Who wants that? The Lord of hosts working *against* them? Not me, that's who.

Life is hard enough when he's with me, working alongside and for me. Why would I ever want the all-powerful God pushing against me? And yet, we return to the admission that we often live our lives in quiet independence from him every day. This is what it means to be proud.

Even when trouble hits, we scramble hard to work our way out of the jam.

As an afterthought, a prayer is offered.

A WORD PICTURE

Listen carefully, for we are close to the answer God has for us. Yes, it will soon entail our hard and righteous work. But first this: *Are we willing to humble ourselves under God's mighty hand?*

What does that even mean?

This is a word picture reaching way back to the Old Testament. For example, it was only the mighty hand of God that compelled Pharaoh to release Israel from bondage.[20] God's strong hand reveals his greatness, for he is like no other.[21] In the middle of a letter about the unimaginable coming toward you, remember God is in control—even of that suffering.

This stirs up questions again, but for now, let's note that the mighty hand of God will protect us. Whatever hardship you now face is not intimidating to him. It is not overwhelming or confusing to him.

When a storm moves in fast, we still have a choice: We can stand proudly like some kind of superhero—hands on our hips, chest out, cape flapping in the wind . . . we can fold like a pup tent in a hurricane . . . we can angrily shake our fist at the howling skies . . . we can bitterly blame the rest of the world while the thunder rolls . . . we can scramble for some quick fix in the driving rain.

Or, we take shelter under the mighty hand of God. We humble ourselves. The most literal translation of the Greek word used here (*tapeinoō*) is "to cause [something or someone] to be at a lower point."[22]

AN UNCOMFORTABLE POSTURE

In Scriptures you'll see people sitting, standing, or kneeling. Sometimes your posture can match your prayers. When I'm worried, I walk with God. Sometimes we pace together and talk it through. When I'm worshiping and thanking him, I look up. When I'm asking for help, I reach up. When I'm confessing, I'm on my knees, hiding my face at first. The Bible also talks of people lying flat on their face before God. There's a great tradition in the ancient church of doing that. I don't do that much, do you?

That's starting to change since I experienced that posture firsthand.

I was the main speaker of a large conference one afternoon. The morning was full of leading breakout sessions, and now it was time to move quickly to the main auditorium. I wanted to get wired up, gather my thoughts, and pray before I spoke.

I was led to a prep room, where I hoped all of this could happen. Not long after, the CEO of the organization sponsoring this event met me back there. After the pleasantries (you want to be nice, right?), I assumed he'd want to collect himself as well since he, too, would be speaking. Enter a young man from South Africa who was emceeing this session. He made sure he had both of our details right for his own peace of mind. No worries. I looked at my watch—plenty of time. At this point, the executive said, "Fellas, I don't know about you, but I need to get on my face before God." We both responded, "Yeah, sounds good; let's pray." At which point he asks us to join him on the floor, on our face before God.

I didn't know he meant that literally.

Now, I've prayed that way before. But not with others. Ever. I started listening to this humble man pour his heart out. Meanwhile, my own prayer had a back-and-forth dialogue to it: "God, please. I'm trying here. But this floor is filthy, and I've got to go out there in a minute." "No, no he's right." (I could hear the longing in the other prayer as it softened my own words.) Then a tech person opened the door abruptly, and who knows what he thought when he saw three guys plastered to the floor. Part of me desperately wanted to get up and explain: "This isn't as weird as it looks. We are all completely sober. I promise."

But then God was taking over.

I began to pray from a different place, confessing my pride that is filthier than anything on that floor. I admitted one more time how I worry too much about what others think of me. But then the gratitude showed up. I thanked God for this opportunity. I thanked him for my family, for my wife, without whom I couldn't imagine doing any of this. I thought about the church God has allowed me to be a part of for so many years, and how I don't deserve a bit of it.

I couldn't wait for what happened next. "God, who cares what I look like or have stuck on me when I speak." And then I thanked him for pulling a prideful man onto the floor alongside a humble one.

I really should spend more time there.

This is the image Peter describes. It is so counterintuitive, it gags our puffed-up selves to consider it. And yet—in the submitting, there is freedom. What a relief to admit we're not that smart or strong or put together. Instead of blustery posturing, we bow down.

We humble ourselves.

ONE MORE UNCOMFORTABLE WORD

Brené Brown is a research professor and author who's written her own share of books—from a different angle, perhaps, than antifragility. She often writes of the power of vulnerability. In her book *Dare to Lead*, she goes back to previous nuggets of gold in her earlier work, what she calls "vulnerability myths."[23] One such myth goes like this: *I don't do vulnerability.*

She would no doubt agree with Mr. Taleb and Peter, Paul, and James that we are exposed to uncertainty, risk, and stress every day. But here's her very good point regarding all that: "You can do vulnerability, or it can do you."[24]

You can own these vulnerable times and learn how to "rumble," as she says, through that experience—aligning your thinking and reactions and words and behaviors with your values. You can do this. Or not. You can own and experience your vulnerability, or you can ignore it and watch it rip through your life anyway.

I believe what Peter is saying in his book is "do vulnerability."

Admit it. Confess it. Cry it out. Lay it before God. Humble yourself. "I can't do this. I cannot solve this on my own." "I don't want to face this alone." One of the specific actions involves "casting all your anxieties on him, because he cares for you."[25]

What words for our anxious age.

There is much practical and biblical wisdom from authors who have addressed the pain of anxiety in depth. Rebekah Lyons invites us to consciously pursue what she describes as "rhythms of renewal God has given us—Rest, Restoration, Connection, and Creation."[26] Notice again the power of intentional choices. You must build these rhythms into your life. For those in the throes of anxiety at peak levels, specific and professional help can and should be sought. But for each of us who've ever watched our thoughts splintered and our breath taken from such trouble, an earlier thought about saying such things out loud still applies.

Lauren Winner reminds us that the desert saints taught "the beginning of renouncing a thought is simply noticing it."[27] So let us name our anxieties as an expression of our humility. Let us cast them to God as an expression of our faith in him. "Here, take this, for it is so much bigger than me . . ."

It could be the pain of your own body not working as it should. The fear of growing old. It could be the heartbreaking grief of watching this happen to a loved one. It could be the ache of loneliness. The sorrow of a relationship in shambles. It could be the pain from rebellion—self-inflicted wounds you are finally going to stop blaming others for. The abuse of another that is not one bit yours to own. The slow-set trap of addiction. The pressure of making ends meet. The freefall of retirement. The ultimate powerlessness of parenting. The frustration of being furloughed or watching your business evaporate in a locked-down world. The suffering that comes from just about every angle.

Are we getting there?

It is time to humble ourselves under the mighty hand of the sovereign God. The God who is not outmatched or outwitted, even when we are. He is still in charge, and remember this: He is still close. Dallas Willard often spoke of people wondering if their prayers went past the ceiling. He implored if only we understood how radically present God is in our world, our prayers making it to the ceiling would be plenty high enough.[28]

And now the rest of it: *He cares for you.*

The Mighty God of the universe is not just in control of this world during the worst storm of your life; he is attending to the details of your life all the time. Part of our choice in these moments is to trust that he will champion us. In a struggle flooded with tears, we choose to humble ourselves to the one who cares.

> Let us name our anxieties as an expression of our humility. Let us cast them to God as an expression of our faith.

BACK TO LIBERIA

This, too, I saw firsthand. I had returned to Liberia. I had returned to an area I'd not seen for over a decade. Those were in the early days of a movement our church helped start called Advent Conspiracy. Along with the call to worship, Christians could celebrate Christmas by giving more relational gifts. Some of the money saved from not overspending would then be given to those in real need. Those initial churches chose to address the water crisis.

This is why I was there all those years ago. I met a village elder who voiced his skepticism of our promise of clean water. Why? Because, in his words, others had made promises in the name of Jesus and never came back. At this point, we had no way of knowing a small step would set off a chain reaction of thousands of churches around the globe celebrating Christmas differently. All we knew back then was that at least this one promise had to be kept. And it was.

I was hoping to see what God had done there after all this time. We found the village, but it was different. Same simple houses. Same red dirt. Same welcoming people. But now there was also laughter and dancing, and mostly what I noticed was children. Healthy, running, playing, singing children who were not there before in such abundance. And this: a beautiful new church in the middle of the village. We gathered there for a rau-cous (and long) celebration. By the end of the day, my heart was so crowded, there wasn't room for one thing more.

But there would have to be.

As we gathered in a huge circle to say good-bye, a few of us learned that two of the people working for Living Water had been in a horrible accident on one of those primitive roads not far from us. One had died immediately, and the other would soon succumb to his injuries.

The next day, our last in Liberia, would be spent in a time of mourning with our brothers and sisters. I watched the solemn assembly form in almost silence. Friends, coworkers, loved ones trying to make sense of it all. Eventually, men and women began to tell stories of these two people so noticeably absent from the room. Tender and constrained laughter touched the circle as they recounted sweet stories. But the tears were never far as each new wave of grief came crashing in.

I was being taught a master class in godly grieving. I watched and heard and then felt in my chest the power of strong men weeping openly. They had weathered a civil war. They had survived Ebola. And now this? Friends doing God's work suddenly dying in an accident?

This was as vulnerable as it gets: Praying out loud and loudly, strong and courageous men crying openly, Scripture readings we could barely stand to hear, grief wrapped in questions, and humble faith beneath it all. And then this: Their decision to worship now, before they felt like it. These men and women were compelled to sing of God's faithfulness with broken voices. I remember a refrain that kept returning through the tears: *God, you are wonderful . . . you are so good.*

And then, when he could bear it no longer, a man still weeping went to grab a drum from outside the building. Now the song had more energy, more power, but no fewer tears. They cried out to God with defiant hope, and I could barely breathe.

Surely this is what it looks like to humble yourself under the mighty hand of God, "that he may lift you up in due time."[29] What time? His time. "After you have suffered a little while, [he] will restore you and make you strong, firm and steadfast."[30]

How long is "a little while?" I don't know. I simply don't know. The true and not easy words of Dan Allender come to mind:

God is not bound by time, nor is our story. We desperately want our situation solved. We want resolution. But God unfolds the plot in his own time.[31]

Until then, we persevere. By his sustenance, we endure the day. And then awaken to face the next one. And on that day, God still cares. In due time, he will lift me up. He will do the same for you.

Bombard heaven with your longings, and trust that he and he alone will bring you to a new place. Beyond surviving. Beyond merely bouncing back. This will be different. More than fragile. More than resilient.

This must be the hope that does not disappoint.

It is now time to say more about this.

FOR PERSONAL REFLECTION

- How resilient are you?
- Where in your life do you need to humble yourself and "take shelter under the mighty hand of God?"

ZAMBEZI OVERLOAD

VICTORIA FALLS DELIVERS on every expectation: a thundering sight to behold in the heart of Africa. If you ever get there, you'll soon notice an apparent lack of personal-injury lawyers, because it is pretty much up to you to not die. No guardrails or warnings keep you from peering over the edge of a 350-plus-foot drop. At the end of a trail of rocks covered with the mist of the falls, you encounter a little sign at the end that warns those rocks are slippery when wet. Thanks for that. If you want to look over the edge? That's your call.

I'm not sure it's that different when you partake of a different adventure a little closer to the water—as in rafting the mighty Zambezi river that falls into that deep gorge[1] and flows eventually to the Indian Ocean. Make no mistake, the people guiding you are quite serious about it all. They'll outfit you and train you for a few minutes in some basic dos and don'ts. What to do when someone falls out or gets washed overboard and something about not panicking in the violent water.

This river is legendary for its rapids—classified by the British Canoe Union (a group that thinks about such things) as "a Grade 5 river with extremely difficult, long and violent rapids, steep gradients, big drops and pressure areas."[2] The guides don't actually read that description to you, but most rafters at this point had their game faces on as we climbed down this steep gorge on ladders made of tree branches.

Once you're at the water's edge and getting into the raft, you learn the names of some of the bigger rapids: "Stairway to Heaven" . . . "Devil's Toilet Bowl" . . . "the Terminator." You'll start off with an easy one, just to warm up. It's called—and I'm not making this up—"The Gnashing Jaws of Death." It sounded much worse than it was, and then we were on our way to "The Three Ugly Sisters" (again, I am not making these names up nor approving of them) and then, their "Mother." These impolite names are used to describe a massive wave train that is moving fast. A train from which I was about to fall off and then under.

A FACE FULL OF RAFT

At some point, the raft pushed up high and to the right. My first real hint of trouble was when my friend Rick, *who used to be sitting to my right,* flew over the top of me and to the left. The whole raft flipped, and then everyone was in the water, scrambling to the surface in this seething cauldron. The first thing that comes to your mind in such moments is the immediate need for oxygen. Since I was on the low side of this flip, when I tried to surface, I found myself underneath the overturned raft.

Not to worry. In that "extensive" orientation, you're told about using air pockets in such rare situations. Catch your breath and push out from under. The air-pocket theory does not apply when the boat itself is getting sucked into a hole of violent water, however. This means when I tried to surface, I was greeted with a face full of raft, but no air.

This left me a little disappointed.

With breathing now moving to the top of my to-do list, I pulled out from under the raft, only to be sucked into one of the infamous whirlpools of the Zambezi. No matter what I did to escape, this river kept pulling me back under.

And then, finally, it spit me out. Or had someone pulled me out? It wasn't very clear at that point.

FAST AND SLOW

It's funny how fast your brain functions in crisis. All the synapses were firing. Rapid thoughts and memories exploded while I focused on the next microsecond to grab a breath. And then I was vacuumed into the vortex again. Wait, I just lost my shoe. How will I hike back out of the gorge without it? Will I even get the chance? Time for another breath.

It's also strange how time slows in these moments.

It seemed like an awfully long time to be trapped in those crashing waves. I thought about our girls (who were NOT with me). I thought about Robin (also not with me) and—how's this for cheery—how I was going to die on our anniversary. Yes, I was going to meet my family later that night to celebrate our anniversary. And now I was praying, "God, please help me . . . I don't want that for Robin."

Have you ever been there?

Maybe it wasn't a mishap in an African river and an overly dramatic prayer about your anniversary. But perhaps you've been in a situation where you really couldn't help yourself. Where you desperately needed God to intervene and things just weren't happening fast enough.

In the previous chapter, we began to see a life that never settles will still involve facing struggles and threats. But the promise of God is that in those moments, we can grow stronger and, by his grace and even because of that hardship, we can emerge as more than we were before. But this process takes time. Peter promised *in due time* God would lift us up.

This means that in those thrashing moments when our brains are on fire and time freezes, we wait.

I can't think of a less fun thing to do.

I can't think of a more necessary thing for us to learn to do.

NOT EASY, JUST WORTH IT

> But they who wait for the LORD shall renew their strength;
> they shall mount up with wings like eagles;
> they shall run and not be weary;
> they shall walk and not faint.
>
> ISAIAH 40:31, ESV

So much wisdom has already been shared about this, a favorite Scripture of many, that I hesitate to go much further. It will be wise at this point to note a modern sage whose thoughts shaped some of my own all those years ago. John Ortberg writes of the difference between what he calls the "fairly trivial" kinds of waiting with which most of us struggle and a deeper, more painful kind of waiting, such as

—The waiting of a single person who hopes God might have marriage in store but is beginning to despair

—The waiting of a childless couple who desperately want to start a family . . .

—The waiting of someone who longs to have work that is meaningful and significant and yet cannot seem to find it . . .[3]

He goes on to quote theologian Lewis Smedes, who saw waiting as "our destiny as creatures who cannot by themselves bring about what they hope for" and wrote,

We wait in the darkness for a flame we cannot light.

We wait in fear for a happy ending we cannot write.

We wait for a not yet that feels like a not ever.

Waiting is the hardest work of hope.[4]

Hope. It's the word we promised to come back to at the end of the last chapter. It will be worth it for us to state a few of the obvious benefits of hope before we move on. Author Daniel Goleman shared many examples of the benefits from what he termed *optimism* in his bestseller *Emotional Intelligence*. One included was a study of 122 men who were evaluated on their optimism and pessimism after their first heart attack.

Eight years later, of the 25 most pessimistic men, 21 had died; of the 25 most optimistic, just 6 had died. Their mental outlook proved a better predictor of survival than any medical risk factor, including the amount of damage to the heart in the first attack, artery blockage, cholesterol level, or blood pressure.

Similar results were reported from patients going into artery bypass surgery. Those who were more optimistic recovered faster and with fewer post-op complications than their pessimistic counterparts. "Like its near cousin optimism," Goleman concludes, "hope has healing power."[5]

The writer of Proverbs agrees. "Hope deferred makes the heart sick, but a longing fulfilled is a tree of life."[6] Hope is more than a "There, there, it'll be all right" pat on your wrist. It infuses our tired souls with life. It strengthens the weak and emboldens the timid. Who doesn't want more hope?

But when Smedes and Ortberg (and Isaiah) connect our hope to waiting, we hold back. When we are told there is a glorious interplay between our waiting and our hope growing—our faith growing deeper—our honest response is "I'm not interested."

In some ways, this makes sense.

It seems only natural to do something—anything—in the middle of the struggle. To flail and fight is what keeps our head above water. Take it from me: You want your head above water. Yet, as others have noted, waiting is not passive. Nor is it avoiding responsibility and hoping things will take care of themselves. Again, Ortberg says it so well: "Waiting on the Lord is a confident, disciplined, expectant, active, and sometimes painful clinging to God."[7]

We want what Isaiah promised: to soar like eagles, to run and not be weary, to at least walk and not faint. We long deep down to survive, but even more, we wonder if all this talk of prevailing and flourishing is more than mere words.

It is.

BRAIDING OUR LIFE TO HIS

Perhaps it will help to focus on the Hebrew word translated here as "wait": *qavah*.

This word conjures up the image of someone pulling and twisting strands together until he or she has braided a strong rope or cord. One strand on its own frays and snaps with the load. Weave it around others, it becomes a rope that can bear the weight it never could on its own. In fact, the noun formed out of this verb is sometimes translated "rope."

Thus, the idea of biblical waiting is binding ourselves, braiding our life together with God's. This is the picture of a relationship with the creator of all things.

The Hebrew concept of faith was a daily, ongoing experience. It was not a formula or a ritual. Faith was not merely an intellectual agreement with some truth claim (though this was certainly part of it). It was—and is for us today—a back-and-forth connection at the deepest layers of our being. Waiting, as so vividly depicted in this verb, is the confident "clinging" to God described above. To wait on the Lord means that you trust him enough to wrap the last frayed strand of your life around his strength.

> To wait on the Lord means that you trust him enough to wrap the last frayed strand of your life around his strength.

And his strength then becomes yours.

This is what relating to God in real time looks like.

No wonder this beautiful word is also translated as "hope." Goleman is right, and the research supports it: "Hope . . . is more than the sunny view that everything will turn out all right."[8]

For those who wait on the Lord, the hope we experience is the active reaching out to the God who is there. Our hope shows up when we wrap that last strand of ourselves around his presence.

DON'T "WAIT" TO WAIT ON HIM

What, then, in a practical sense, does this look like? We stew in a sour soup of emotions for far too long before coming to God. For some, it is the crazy notion of getting ourselves in a better condition to approach him. (As if our current situation and subsequent reaction will be a shock.) Oftentimes, in these harried moments, we start strategizing what should and will happen next. Before long, we're moving fast again, forcing our agenda and our solutions into the mix.

Interestingly enough, this can bring some relief in the short term. That's why we do it. It feels good to be in control of something again. But this isn't the true way out. Instead, with the decision-making part of your brain, do just that. It's time for another choice. Even the act of making a decision begins to change our brain chemistry, allowing for better focus, reducing worry and—get this—making the next decision becomes easier. "Research shows that decisiveness in one part of your life can improve your decisiveness in other parts of your life."[9]

Put this phenomenon to good use. Now that you're clear on how active biblical waiting is, make a conscious choice to do just that. Know what you're doing. Notice what you're doing. When the raft is upended and it's hard to know the next right thing to do, come back to what you've already seen is right.

HANG ON TO HIS WORDS

Reading Scripture is one of the most tangible forms of reaching out to God. Remember the chain reaction set off by the power of the story. Many who read those words a few chapters ago would agree that this would be "good for us." Most who call themselves Christians would casually agree to this. And yet, we don't much with the Bible. As few as 19 percent of churchgoers personally read the Bible daily.[10] This is still not the time to pile guilt on top of despair. (Does that ever work?) But neither can we ignore this most important act of seeking God.

Some of the previous points start coming together now:

Start small. By committing to reading the Bible in small doses (there are many strategies available to you), you have a better chance. Try this once a day (or three times a week, for that matter, just try this) for three weeks, and see if it's worth it. Don't expect to do this perfectly—you probably won't. But do it.

Watch for the chain reaction. Alex Korb, a neuroscientist at UCLA and author of *The Upward Spiral*, explains that "the dorsal striatum [the part of your brain where the ruts of your habits are formed] responds to repetition." He continues: "It doesn't matter if you want to do something—every single time you do it, it gets further wired into [it]."[11] Of course, it helps when you want to do a thing and you even see it as something you value greatly.

The point is, new ruts can furrow into our brains. Momentum can build, and the benefits are real. When we habitually braid our thoughts to the word of God, our thoughts become clearer and our emotions run less rampant than before, especially in times of great stress. This becomes a reliable way to hear his voice above the din. Those who have entered the dark and rough waves ahead of us provide another clue to reaching out.

> Reading Scripture is one of the most tangible forms of reaching out to God.

NOW USE YOUR WORDS (AGAIN)

Are you noticing a theme here? Cry out to God. And as best you can, use words. It might start off as simple as the Breton Fisherman's Prayer, which was shared with new submarine captains by Admiral Hyman Rickover. He then famously gave the same prayer to President Kennedy, who kept the plaque on his desk in the Oval Office.

O God, Thy sea is so great and my boat is so small.[12]

No kidding.

Now go further as you reach up for his help. In the Scriptures, we encounter all manner of questions and cries being tossed God's way—not by skeptics or enemies of God, but by those who trust him. David comes to mind. Jesus, of course. So, too, the heartbroken Jeremiah, who was given an almost unbearable assignment to speak hard and frightening words to a people he loved, a people who hated him for it. God had called him to this role, so sometimes pouring his heart out was all he could do:

> **Jeremiah:** O Eternal One—You know what I am facing;
>   Remember me, and pay attention to my plight . . .
> So why does my pain never end?
>   Why does this wound never heal?
> Will you be to me as deceptive and unreliable as a dry
>   stream to a thirsty man?[13]

Talk about using your own words. Jeremiah felt the freedom to pour out his heart to the God who is big enough for our fears and frustrations. This was not a one-way conversation. As he cried out, he also listened. In the expression of these hurts, something began to happen: Jeremiah's strength was renewed.

This wasn't simply a matter of getting it out of his system. In our crying out, we articulate the fear and hurt more specifically. No longer is it a cloud we are wrestling with. This alone makes the struggle more tangible. In a study aptly titled "Putting Feelings into Words," researchers discovered the mere act of naming your emotions activates the "thinking" (prefrontal cortex) part of your brain and tones down the reactions from the "emotional" (limbic) system.[14]

No longer a blurry threat, you've formed words as to what it is that you're facing and fearing. Even if you don't have specific notions of what you need next. Think of these specific and not-always-pretty prayers as part of you wrapping yourself around God's strength.

But what about when there are no words?

TOO DEEP FOR WORDS

Another blessed promise from Romans 8 comes into play. Paul says that on this groaning planet, we will *groan inwardly*. He also admits what we've come to know ourselves: Sometimes in the groaning we don't know what to pray. When you are out of words, out of options, and fast running out of hope, choose to reach out anyway.

Our triune God enters the hurt and fallenness of it all in ways that defy description (or research). The Holy Spirit will intercede in those weak and waiting breaths.

> In the same way, the Spirit helps us in our weakness. We
> do not know what we ought to pray for, but the Spirit
> himself intercedes for us through wordless groans.[15]

He will go before the Father concerning this situation we can't yet explain, groaning on our behalf when matters are too deep for words. This is the work of the Holy Spirit, and he is closer than your next breath.

In the waiting weighed down with worry, God is there. In the fear, God is there. In the creeping sadness, God is there. In the confusion and fear, God is there. Not just in the aftermath to put the pieces back together, but in the middle of the storm.

NOW, NOT LATER

I will never forget how God taught me that lesson in a moment I almost missed. A few years ago, I was about to conduct a funeral, and I was begging God for all the wisdom and grace he was willing to afford me.

The room at our main campus was packed. Tragedy had ripped through our community. The team had prayerfully and thoughtfully put a service together that would honor everyone. Music had been selected. My stories and Scriptures were ready. I'd prayed with the parents and their remaining daughter. Now it was time for us to walk into a room with two coffins. God help me. God help us.

I was doing what I thought I was supposed to do—walk the

family into a room they dreaded entering and trust God would meet us . . . there. That's when the mom gently reached out, grabbed my arm, and said, "Greg, you're walking too fast."

I hadn't considered what the poet John O'Donohue called "the ruin of absence."[16] Here was a family ruined and about to walk into the ruins left by the absence of teenage daughters. I was trying my best to imagine the dread of it all, but still, I was moving too fast.

I wasn't trying to gloss over the pain. We had and would continue admitting all that was crumbling around us. But I so wanted them to know God was waiting for them around that next horrible corner. And he was there in that painful, gospel-filled service: God did sustain us all, most beautifully that family. He is faithful, and he is not finished with them.

The mistake I was making until gently corrected was simply this: In my desire for them to know God was in the future, I forgot that what this grieving mom needed was God much sooner than in the next room. She needed him in the present.

> Often, God will whisper—if nothing else, that he knows. That he's there.

In the following minutes, we preached the promise of the Resurrection and the hope of those who have trusted in him. This is very good news indeed. God will meet you there in that future, and it will be something.

But until then, every step of the way, God will meet you here. Now.

Even when words fail us.

In that silence, listen. For often, God will whisper—if nothing else, that he knows. That he's there. In this back-and-forth between the two of you, there will be moments of complaint or panic, followed by a faith that seeps back into your heart. Just a few verses after Jeremiah questions God so boldly, he prays these words: "O Eternal One, You are my strength, my fortress, my sanctuary in times of trouble."[17]

Is this the same person? Yes, of course. Who among us hasn't felt that woozy swing from one extreme to another? But it is here that God meets us—in the middle of our fatigue giving way to fatalism, he's close. And as we reach out, something begins to happen.

For Jeremiah (and the rest of us), it might begin with another conscious decision.

YOUR MOTHER KNEW WHAT SHE WAS DOING

Your mother taught you to say "thank you" as part of an overall, good-mannered approach to life. What specific studies in the areas of neuroscience have discovered is that gratitude is more than being polite. It's good for you. Benefits include improved moods, reduced worry, feeling more connected to others, improved sleep, better physical health, and being more likely to engage in healthy activities.[18]

It's a part of thriving in this world. And yet, it sounds so obvious, you can't believe this is a part of clinging to God.

First a word about all this brain science. A question might be posed: Do scientific discoveries about how we think, feel, and respond in times of crisis take away from the beauty of God's Word? Not one bit. He is, after all, the same Creator who *knit you together in your mother's womb*—fearfully and wonderfully so.[19]

Hopefully such references to how our brains work will serve as handles for appreciating the practical wisdom of God's Word. They might also motivate the less inclined. Every bit of this points back to our glorious God, who knows how a flourishing, thriving, not-settling-for-less life works. These are not tricks. They work because God made us this way and he knows what he's doing.

He also knows what will happen when we practice gratitude.

It is an integral way we wrap ourselves around his strength.

DON'T JUST COUNT 'EM, NAME 'EM

Lyrics emerge from a childhood of singing hymns I didn't much like or appreciate. At first, it's hard to give this one much thought because of the countless times I heard it:

> *When upon life's billows you are tempest-tossed,*
> *When you are discouraged, thinking all is lost,*
> *Count your many blessings, name them one by one,*
> *And it will surprise you what the Lord has done.*[20]

The tune may not work for me, but the words are spot on: It's important to name your blessings. Perhaps in a journal. Perhaps as a morning routine. Certainly in our prayers and in our conversations wherein we celebrate God. With trusting determination, we set our gaze on that for which we are grateful. Even getting in the habit of looking for something is something. Korb writes:

> Remembering to be grateful is a form of emotional intelligence. One study found that it actually affected neuron density in [key regions of] the prefrontal cortex. These density changes suggest that as emotional intelligence increases, the neurons in these areas become more efficient. With higher emotional intelligence, it simply takes less effort to be grateful.[21]

Even in Jeremiah's heartache, he came back to the faithfulness of Yahweh. It had become habit. Part of what God was teaching Israel and her prophets was that gratitude is not only an antidote to worry. It is a fundamental ingredient to enduring, this act of recalling and recounting the many blessings from the Eternal One who had lavished his love on them.

This is why Israel was called again and again to remember the great act of redemption that anchors the Hebrew Scriptures. The story of the Exodus is the greatest blessing they'd ever received as a people. Without it, their history would fade into obscurity. As a nation, they were instructed again and again to remember and retell the story of their rescue.

All throughout the Exodus story, the verbs are active and physical and dramatic. It is God who's doing all the work. Back in the middle of the struggle between Pharaoh and Moses in Exodus 6, God says "I will free you from being slaves . . . I will redeem you with an outstretched arm . . ."[22] The word translated as *free* has a kind of abruptness to it in the Hebrew.[23] It is the picture of physically grabbing someone to pull them out of danger.

And he will do this with an outstretched arm.

SNATCHED FROM DANGER

I was in a bad way, in a violent river, being sucked into one of those crashing holes of water, and I couldn't escape. Yet here I was. Did the whirlpool spit me out? Or had someone pulled me out of trouble?

It was our guide, Timba, who grabbed me and brought me up and toward our raft.

By then, everyone else was back at this overturned raft, hanging on for dear life. And now I was too.

I was so overwhelmed with relief and gratitude, and with more than a little adrenaline rushing through my veins. We really weren't out of trouble yet, but we had a break in the action. I was trying to fill Timba in on what had just happened. He listened, smiled, and then said, "I know. I saw the whole thing. You were trapped under the raft and then sucked into that whirlpool. I saw you go down each time. I knew right where you were. I was just waiting for the right moment to snatch you out of there."

The God who loves me leaned a bit more on my shoulders in the middle of that heart-pumping adventure. I didn't hear an audible voice, but God spoke to me, and it went something like this: "Are you getting this, son, or do I need to make it even more obvious? I see it all. Every time. And I'm right here."

He is the God who has already redeemed me with his out-stretched arm, and still I forget.

How many times have I felt completely out of options? Drowning, really, in the chaos of a hard season? I've even convinced myself no one else can see what I'm going through, much less appreciate the weight of it all. But God does. He's never once taken his eye off me.

"I've got you, son. I saw the whole thing . . . I was just waiting for the right moment to snatch you out of there."

> There is a faith that endures, a hope that will not disappoint.

I do not know what you are facing. But I know the God who sees everything. I know the God who rescues. He knows what pulls you under these days. That struggle. That obstacle. That heartache. That fear. That loneliness or regret or unbelievable burden. He is saddened, but not frightened. Attentive, but not overwhelmed. And he is close.

The life that never settles will still face trouble.

But there is a faith that endures, a hope that will not disappoint. Those that wait on the Lord, those who wrap the last frayed strand of themselves around the strong arm of our mighty God, will not be disappointed. They'll walk again. Run. Sometimes even soar.

FOR PERSONAL REFLECTION

- When was the last time you felt like you were drowning in life?
- Name one thing that brought you joy today. Give thanks to God.

10

MUPPETS IN THE BALCONY

NOW THAT WE'VE STARTED TALKING about hope, what's one hope you have—for you, your friends, family, church, community, or the world? Did a specific thought or dream come to mind? Or did you roll your eyes and think, *Here comes the rah-rah speech*? If the question had been, "Tell me what's *wrong* with you, your friends, et cetera," answers would by flying through your head right now.

Ah, but that wasn't the question.

When you hear yourself or others speak of hope for this world, what's your first reaction? When you read of some effort of an individual or group trying to make things better, what thought first shows up in your head? When you see people actually doing something in the church, the community, the world, what words fall out of your mouth easily?

Would you make Statler and Waldorf proud?

Depending on your age or your exposure to pop culture, you may not know them by name. You may not even recognize this description, for the origin of this dyspeptic duo reaches all the way back to the almost-ancient era known as the 1970s.

For starters, they're Muppets.

They were a part of the original Muppets show and since then have found their way into everything from movies to a Marvel comic book appearance[1] to commercials for a Facebook product.

They are the two old guys up in the balcony.

Cranky, sarcastic, and never satisfied, these two never have anything good to say. Laughing, mocking, and generally lobbing one-liners at everyone else, they comment on how the show is going.

But they are always spectators.

It's funny to watch—until we see it in real life. Our world has developed quite the habit for critiquing anyone trying to get things done in this world. Still learning how to steward our new-ish connectivity on the planet, many eagerly jump on a bigger soapbox, sharing all that they see everyone else doing . . . *wrong.*

Is it fair to say each of us is a snarky comment or two away from being a Muppet in the balcony?

To be sure, these decidedly hope-starved times lure many to these harsher tones. They cannot see or name one good thing God has done, such is their spiritual blindness. To hope (or wait) for him to do the next good thing is beyond their tired imaginations. For those of us who are beginning to say out loud that God is not finished with us or the rest of creation, what's our excuse?

Cynical thoughts still tease out our ugly words far too easily.

The writer of Proverbs has a thought that might help (or offend):

> Fools find no pleasure in understanding
>> but delight in airing their own opinions.[2]

Let's memorize this one together, shall we?

We live in an age that delights in the airing of opinions. We also run the risk of being molded by this delight. The dangerous blend of big data and small vision has lulled the followers of Jesus into a trap. We have become addicted to the sound of our voices and the sight of our own words.

> Our world has developed quite the habit for critiquing anyone trying to get things done.

Along the way, we settle for a luke-warminess that leads to grumpiness.

"Yes," the more vocal will say, "but how could our hearts not stir with righteous indignation when we read the latest headline from our newsfeed or see a clip on YouTube about *that* political party?" Should we not be upset when we are updated on Facebook on a particular issue? To put it more personally, what I often hear is something like this:

- "I get so angry when I see and hear what is happening in our world, what do you expect me to do—*nothing?*"
- "When I post something, it's my way of pushing back on _____ (*fill in the blank with whomever sits on the other side of whatever divide*)."
- "If we stay silent, they will win."

And so we fling our opinions into cyberspace. Does this accomplish much good in God's world? Does it do our insides as much good as we might assume? Do we even understand what is happening when we scream from the balcony?

USHERED INTO THE TRAP

First, like Statler and Waldorf, it is important to know we are mostly screaming to other angry Muppets. We tend to seek out information and viewpoints that line up with our own.

Researchers refer to this as "selective exposure."[3] We avoid that which challenges our thinking. Some of this is intentional, but some of it is happening without our knowledge. Professor C Thi Nguyen summarizes this phenomenon well with an example of what happens when we get our news from Facebook feeds and other social media:

> Our Facebook feed consists mostly of our friends and colleagues, the majority of whom share our own political and cultural views. We visit our favourite like-minded blogs and websites. At the same time, various algorithms behind the scenes, such as those inside Google search, invisibly personalise our searches, making it more likely that we'll see only what we want to see.[4]

For the sake of our convenience and not drowning in the overflow of information that is the Internet, we now allow a form of artificial intelligence (say, Google and Facebook's algorithms) to filter out all those things we either might not be interested in or—and here's the real point—we might not agree with. In these "bubbles," as they are called,[5] we "encounter exaggerated amounts of agreement and suppressed levels of disagreement."[6]

What's wrong with that?

We tend to like being around people who like what we like. And why not? It's easier and more enjoyable, so we think. But in the age of interconnectivity and massive data collection, it becomes more than who we hang out with on the weekend. This is no longer a conversation across the backyard fence, in the lobby at church, or, for that matter, at the corner pub. Our interactions are being carefully and quietly sculpted, even as we're steered toward articles (and other people) we might like.

Without even knowing it, we've been led into a box in the balcony to sit with those who think like us.

From here, we blast out our sentiments just to hear them echo back from others in this chamber who think like us. Learning something from a different perspective becomes secondary to having the people in my box agree with me. Along the way, we become emboldened with these exaggerated levels of agreement and are increasingly convinced of how right we are. We are now in a cycle. The uglier the tone, the more "attaboys" (or "attagirls") we hear, which only leads to more ugliness. Couple that with the outrage focused at anyone who dares to voice a disagreement in that bubble, and the trap is set. Disagreement is mostly muted in this bubble created around us. Soon we cannot imagine any sane—*or Jesus-loving person*—not agreeing with us.

And before you know it, we're Muppets in a balcony.

This accomplishes so very little. To be clear, the state of our world is worth our concern—and, at times, indignation. The great challenge for the followers of Christ is the question: *What shall we do?* Merely offer more scathing critiques? No. Impelled less by our outrage and more by the outreach of God's love, it is time to take action. Our love (if it is that) must now move from word to deed.

The great British pastor John Stott said it quite forcefully:

> When society does go bad, we Christians tend to throw up our hands in pious horror and reproach the non-Christian world; but should we not rather reproach ourselves? One can hardly blame unsalted meat for going bad. It cannot do anything else. The real question to ask is: where is the salt?[7]

Let's stay with our original example just a bit longer. If you find yourself caught in a closed loop of anger, lobbing one grenade of hate after another, try this: Jump out of the balcony. Or at least excuse yourself from it and find your way down to where the real action is.

BREAKING OUT

To escape this cycle and move into real difference-making will require a concerted effort. Now that we know a bit of what is happening behind our computer or phone screens, we should be more careful. The following are a few ways to break out of these artificial bubbles:

Watch your diet. No, not that one. I'm referring to your daily consumption of information. One oft-cited number puts our daily production of new data at 2.5 quintillion bytes (that's a billion billion bytes).[8] This is, of course, more than anyone can keep up with. It only makes sense that we pick and choose what new information we will ingest. Out of habit and convenience, we usually narrow our sources down. In the same way fast food offers instant gratification with less substance, a quick headline or angry tweet rarely offers solid information. Some issues and stories require more "bytes," and some require less. The occasional fast will also prove to be healthy.

Be a savvy consumer. Stay aware of this new way you are being presented information. Check a source. Ask one more question about why this story landed in your news feed or that search yielded those results. The "Internet of things" means all your devices and objects that make your life easier are also being used to show you more of what you want. That is not always a good thing.

Do a deeper dive. On issues where your passions ignite, more research will be worth it. Remembering the above, now push past what's being presented to learn more. Become conversant with a differing viewpoint. Pray for understanding (and lower blood pressure) as you try to discern how someone could arrive at such a different conclusion from you.

Guard against demonizing. From a distance, it becomes easy to perceive (and treat) those with whom we disagree as "a threat, an enemy, a monster."[9] More of an "it" than a person. Watch how easily our rhetoric dehumanizes in these settings. Ad hominem attacks and childish name-calling—much less proud pronouncements of someone's damnation—are not the way of Jesus.

When you move from the balcony, you'll be better equipped to soon join real people already in the real world. And in the process, you'll make a conscious choice to reject one of the newer lures of our day.

AN ODD AND UNCOMFORTABLE WORD

Slacktivism. No longer a new term, it is the combination of two words: *slacker* and *activism.* At first glance, they don't really fit together, do they? How can one be *active* in the world, trying to solve a problem, while still being referred to as a *slacker*? And yet, this unfortunate term described an emerging phenomenon several years ago: those using the Internet to "support an issue or social cause *involving virtually no effort*"[10] on their part. Such activity can be loud and blustery, but it happens from afar, sitting on the couch, and costs nothing.

It is time to reject the temptation to feel a little better about ourselves because we liked or retweeted a zinger about some headline, problem, or public figure. This will accomplish little. If you want to do something shockingly good, get into the thick of what God is still doing in this world.

Far too many people are marginalized not by the efforts of a vast conspiracy, but out of their own decision to merely provide color commentary from the sidelines. Settle for the margins no longer. Take that definitive step on your journey, fraught with its own risks, and move onto the stage.

Strange and wondrous things will soon happen. From such a nontheoretical vantage point, God's work is done. Knowledge of what is hard and worth doing in this world seeps into our prideful thoughts. We begin to know what we don't know. The distance that has demonized others begins to close. New allies

> If you want to do something shockingly good, get into the thick of what God is still doing in this world.

are forged from old rivalries. Even our words are now pruned out of respect and newfound wisdom.[11]

Ironically, the lean-and-not-so-mean version of our opinions are heard with more weight by more people to more effect. This is the stunning moment when you begin to find your story in the grand story. Wondrous things indeed, with one caveat:

You still have to jump.

FOR SUCH A TIME AS THIS

The details surrounding the tale of Esther take us into the strange and misogynistic ways of an ancient culture. The Jewish people had been living in exile for many years. Now they were under the authority of a Persian ruler who allowed some to return to their homeland. It was in this era that a young (Jewish) woman still living in Persia was selected to marry the mighty King Xerxes, commander of the vast army who would fight the Spartans at Thermopylae. After banishing his previous queen in a selfish tantrum, a beauty contest to find her replacement was formed—including cosmetic treatments for all the contestants living in his harem so they could look their best for the king. Like I said, strange and misogynistic.

Details of political intrigue, a bitter rivalry laced with anti-Semitism, a foiled assassination plot, and the hidden nature of Esther's true heritage are all mentioned in the early chapters of this book with her name. In later chapters, the plot points come rushing together: That bitter rivalry between her uncle and a member of the administration resulted in a plan to exterminate the Jewish people "on a single day, the thirteenth day of the twelfth month."[12]

When the day of this pogrom became known publicly, Israel wept (and for good reason). Cousin Mordecai gets word to Queen Esther and pleads with her to intervene before the massacre takes place. Perhaps the king would listen to his beautiful bride. At first, she offers a worrisome reason for not getting involved. His strong reply includes a warning that God will rescue his people with or without her. And then, this famous admonition: "Who knows but that you have come to your royal position *for such a time as this?*"[13]

Esther, this is your time. Don't miss a chance to see God at work. Get involved.

It took a nudge, but she did. And with her intervention, the genocidal decree was repealed and those wanting such evil were vanquished. Still, the queen had to step into this situation.

Why did she hesitate? Because getting involved involves risk. What if she was misunderstood? What if this fickle and powerful ruler was in a bad mood? And (here's the real issue): What if she would now be persecuted as well? It would be so much easier—or so she thought—to do nothing and enjoy life as the queen. Perhaps from a safe distance, she could comment on what a shame the whole situation had become.

But she'd still be queen.

Note that her fears were legitimate: approaching the king without an invitation usually carried a sentence of death. While not always as high a cost, getting involved always carries a risk. Esther would have to risk her standing and her safety to draw the king's attention to this horror-in-the-making. In the end, the strong words of Mordecai awakened her to the calling on her life.

It was no accident Esther found herself so close to power (the implication here is the sovereign God of Israel had arranged all of this)—*for such a time as this.* To her credit, she wisely called the Jewish people to prayer, for God doesn't ask us to take a step without his help. And then, with courageous determination ("If

I perish, I perish") and the fate of her own people hanging in the balance, Esther finally steps into the moment.

And her people are saved.

SAME COURAGE, DIFFERENT KING

Before the Jewish people were taken into that exile, a faithful prophet we've already met was warning his nation it would happen. Few believed Jeremiah, and even fewer wanted to hear his dire predictions (though he's about to be proven right). To silence him, the princes and nobles falsely accuse him of treason to Judah's king. As in the previous story, the king allows his advisors to do as they please. These incensed officials accost Jeremiah and throw him into a cistern in the court of the guard. Here, the rejected prophet disappears into the dark, sinking into the mud. Finally, he is silenced. Soon, he would be dead.

Talk about suppressed levels of disagreement.

But another official in the palace, Ebed-Melech, hears of this injustice. And now it is his turn to do something. We're told he comes from a kingdom we would know as Ethiopia. He, too, was an outsider living on the inside of power. He, too, had much to lose in this moment—his influence, position, perhaps his ability to stay in Jerusalem. Would he now be endangering his own life by standing up for the accused?

As earlier, the option of merely shaking his head from a distance was the easy play.

Instead, he jumps in.

He goes to the king: "Do you know what some of your court officials have done? They have done a wicked thing to Jeremiah the prophet."[14] After speaking truth, this court official from Africa—not Jerusalem—secures permission from the king to rescue Jeremiah. With ropes and rags thrown into that dark hole, the prophet is pulled to safety. The great prophet will live another day to speak for the Lord.

Dramatic stories to be sure. Almost too dramatic. What could we possibly have in common with them?

A FAMILIAR FOE: FEAR

There is a reason "Fear not" is such a regular command from God. It's never far from any of us. In both stories, fear was no doubt faced. In both instances, the risks of getting involved were real. For us, the fears and risks are equally real, if not always life-threatening.

We fear becoming the next target. The air we breathe these days is thick with threat, and the ground is strewn with rocks to hurl at each other's heads. If we take a stand, will we be the next one canceled? Doxxed? Shunned? The loss of standing in a group may be the price exacted for standing up. The loss of position, even relationship, may loom in the distance. Such concerns are well-founded, though often not as disastrous as we fear. Nevertheless, bad things might come our way. No less an expert than Jesus spoke of crosses and the world hating us because it hated him.[15]

It's true, of course. *The very minute you stand against injustice, you can expect some.*

This is the time to pray. Pray for eyes that see all that is true (and not true), all that will last (and not), all that God is doing (and will yet accomplish) in this moment. It's time to pray one more time for better spiritual vision. But also for courage. The threats we face are not always as menacing as we first imagined, but they threaten us nonetheless.

And then ask others to pray for you.

Pray also for me, that whenever I speak, words may
be given me so that I will fearlessly make known the
mystery of the gospel, for which I am an ambassador in
chains. Pray that I may declare it fearlessly, as I should.[16]

If the outspoken Paul had moments he needed help in facing fears, we are in very good company when asking for courage.

We avoid the uncomfortable. In 1910, former president Theodore Roosevelt gave a speech in the Sorbonne in Paris. By all accounts, "Citizenship in a Republic" was a smashing success, though nobody remembered the title of the speech. Most people have since referred to it as "The Man in the Arena" speech for this oft-quoted passage:

> It is not the critic who counts; not the man who points out how the strong man stumbles, or where the doer of deeds could have done them better. The credit belongs to the man who is actually in the arena, whose face is marred by dust and sweat . . .

Less known is the previous paragraph, which holds these timely words:

> The poorest way to face life is to face it with a sneer. There are many men who feel a kind of twisted pride in cynicism; there are many who confine themselves to criticism of the way others do what they themselves dare not even attempt.[17]

Such critics comfortably view the action perched high above the fray on cushy, safe seats in the balcony. They have grown too amused with their sneering, too twisted by their pride.

The constant critique of those actually doing something has now become habit. A cynical habit of thought and speech, a readiness to criticize work which the critic himself never tries to perform, "an intellectual aloofness which will not accept contact with life's realities."[18]

We avoid the discomfort of "contact with life's realities."

The God who stepped out of glory and into this tragedy-of-our-making now bids us to follow him. The same Jesus who endured the cross is calling us to more than the shaking of heads and merely tsk-tsking our disapproval. It's time to plant our feet in the world and get our hands dirty, even if our hearts are broken along the way.

A COMMON QUESTION: AM I UP TO THE CHALLENGE?

There is a moment most of us face when flying. Unless you are one of the lucky few, you will proceed past those already sitting in the wider seats with all the leg room, sipping a cold beverage as they flip through the latest pages of *Architectural Digest*. You only have to do this a few times to figure out the routine: Keep moving. Don't make eye contact. Find your seat in the next cabin. Don't use their overhead compartments. Try not to use too much of their air. These are special people who should not be bothered.

> The God who stepped out of glory and into this tragedy-of-our-making now bids us to follow him.

My youngest, Tori, was very young at the time of this particular flight. She was old enough to have her own little backpack with her "essentials" slung over her shoulder as we walked through first class. She looked like my little world-wizened explorer leading the way. She must've felt that way, too, for she turned midstep through the special people and matter-of-factly asked, for all of them to hear: "So . . . Dad, are we flying in second class again?"

While everyone giggled, I assured her under my breath. "We're not second class, honey, we're coach people."

For the record, you are not second class either.

What God has in mind for you is exactly what you were meant to do. He has—and will—equip you for that assignment as his image-bearer, whether you make it into some hall of fame or not. Not only has he saved you by his grace, but he has something in mind:

> For we are God's handiwork, created in Christ Jesus to do good works, which God prepared in advance for us to do.[19]

From the beginning God had something for you to do in this world he loves. And with that in mind, God has done such an exquisite thing that Paul calls you the "handiwork" of God. The Jerusalem Bible translates this beautiful word as "work of art."[20] You are God's work of art, and that is anything but second class. Your call into the mix may look different than that of those around you, but it is no less important. To believe such lies will starve your days of significance and leave you with little else to do (or so the evil one will soon have you believing) but to comment from the balcony.

A COMMON WORRY: AM I DOING ENOUGH?

Even with the previous truth fresh in our minds, a familiar doubt lingers that our everyday effort has little impact on the great matters of the Kingdom.

This entire book has been an attempt to jostle us out of the mediocre and humdrum. From Jesus himself we have heard how distasteful it is for his followers to settle for so much less. We were made to make a difference.

But does that always mean starting our own nonprofit or packing up and moving elsewhere?

A few years ago, Anthony Bradley, a professor at The King's College, wrote rather forcefully of what he termed "the new legalism." Simply put, he suggested that in recent years the call for particularly younger Christians to be "radical" and "missional" had led to a sad development. He wrote:

I continue to be amazed by the number of youth and young adults who are stressed and burnt out from the regular shaming and feelings of inadequacy if they happen to not be doing something unique and special.

His take on how we arrived at such a place is thought-provoking, whether you agree with his conclusions or not. At one point, he references "a well-intentioned attempt to address lukewarm Christians in the suburbs" but suggests such books, sermons, and movements have produced:

> the sad result . . . that many young adults feel ashamed if they "settle" into ordinary jobs, get married early and start families, live in small towns, or as 1 Thess 4:11 says, "aspire to live quietly, and to mind [their] affairs, and to work with [their] hands."[21]

Is he correct? The anecdotal evidence should at least warn us of the danger of devaluing one's calling based on a few broad metrics. Should anyone assume they have "settled" if they take an "ordinary" job and start their family somewhere outside of a big city? Of course not. There is no compromise in that choice *unless God has called them to do otherwise.* If so, the rumblings of a holy unrest should be heeded. Holy Spirit-weighted conviction is often the prelude to the repentance that leads to freedom.

A step taken only to comply with someone else's stereotypical expectation of the "missional" or "difference-making" life, however, is a step back toward lukewarminess. The Kingdom is too big and God's handiwork is too beautiful for each of us to fit neatly into a one-size-fits-all mold.

This will not look the same for each of us.

It will not boil down to limited zip codes in which we live or worship. This life is not reduced to a short list of vocations and organizations. Beware such lies that bring us to pride on the one hand and a neutered sense of worth on the other.

Those lies also lead to ugly words and hesitant Christians stuck in the balcony.

You may fly in coach with the rest of us, but you are not second class. Neither is your calling. The work is important enough because he is important enough. And this: You are his handiwork. This gives dignity to your work and power to those everyday moments. Paul says elsewhere to do whatever you do for God's glory.[22] And then this: "Always give yourselves fully to the work of the Lord, because you know that your labor in the Lord is not in vain."[23]

Not all will be called to save an entire nation. Not all will confront a king to save a prophet. But you are invited into the work of God. And none of it is ever in vain. The glamorous and hidden, the mega and the micro, Sundays and Thursdays, suburbs and cities, to paraphrase Abraham Kuyper, it's all God's, and it all matters.[24]

With a profound sense of calling and God-given meaning, it is time to resist the algorithms and step out of the echo chambers. It is time to listen well. To stop sneering. To measure our words. To engage in the world around us. May the crucible of today's struggle produce God-inspired creativity for tomorrow's world. New ideas. Outrageous goals. Bighearted dreams. The time is now for kingdom-sized hope to lead the way.

We have been called by Jesus, and that is enough. For he is enough. His Spirit breathes life into our sin-deadened souls. His words ring true in our ears. His life marks the way. How could we settle for resembling hollowed-out puppets with grumpy eyebrows when we can live this life instead?

It's time to crawl, walk, or sometimes jump out of the balcony. There's work to do.

FOR PERSONAL REFLECTION

- Think back on the conversations you had today, in person and online. Were you soothing and refreshing or critical and sarcastic?
- Name one area of your life where you contribute to the noise and cynicism. Ask for God's forgiveness.

WELCOME ABOARD

"WELCOME ABOARD!" These are the words a little boy said to Robin and me, seemingly out of the blue. We had just boarded the plane and were already seated, in our own pretakeoff, get-ready-for-a-three-hour-flight mode. (And no, I wasn't thumbing through *Architectural Digest*, sipping a cool drink.) Then, as this boy and his mom were walking past us in that crowded shuffle, he stopped abruptly at our row and welcomed us.

Just us.

Without missing a beat, he looked up at mom for approval and grinned. I don't know if he'd been told to be nice or this was just his normal approach to flying. The knowing smile on her face hinted that this was not the first time her son had done something special.

Perhaps there was more to his story. Perhaps he was learning how to navigate a big world full of strangers. Or perhaps he didn't even realize yet how wonderfully, shockingly different that moment was.

It was as if God spoke to my heart through that little boy.

I had just been welcomed aboard.

That simple greeting got me thinking . . . *How many times could I be the person who enters a room with a different attitude? How many times could my words and actions be used better to . . .*

- fill the air with soft words?
- gently surprise another with a kind gesture?
- turn the volume of this world down just a notch?
- welcome someone?

RECEIVING ONE ANOTHER

Welcome one another as Christ has welcomed you, for the glory of God.
ROMANS 15:7, ESV

The word Paul uses[1] certainly means "welcome," but it can also be rendered "receive," as in taking someone into your presence, your home, your friendship. *As Christ welcomed (or received) you . . .* What a standard. How exactly did he welcome you? Was it a provisional acceptance? ("Go clean up your life, and then come back.") Were you on probation? ("Let's see how this works out.") Was it packaged with never-ending guilt? ("You're on board, but I'll never let you forget that you shouldn't be.")

How did Christ receive you?

We know the correct answer—with lavish grace and open-armed love. With this verse, Paul reminds us of the standard. How many times could my words and actions reflect this love? How often could my welcoming ways be shockingly, soothingly different? The honest answer is *every day*. This could be the rhythm and cadence of my life. And yet, it often isn't.

On this, I'm not alone.

My previous book (wait—there's another book?) opened with these words:

> We have forgotten how to get along. Some will suggest
> this is nothing new—and they would be right. From
> the first moment of rebellion against a loving God, the
> cracks appeared in our relationships. Ever since, our
> ugly unlovingness has chipped and jackhammered at the
> beauty of God's creation.[2]

I'm not sure things have changed since those words were written. We live in an increasingly hostile world. The landscape is littered with the ghosts of old friendships and artifacts of past failures. Tiptoeing through the rubble, we are reminded of how cautious our next step should be. Disaster awaits at every turn. Fear and rage trade turns driving the conversation; meanwhile, old wounds fester and new hope fades.

We are in this world together, but it does not appear we like it much. Being together, I mean.

This collective retreat from each other exacts a toll. While many social commentators have spoken to this trend fast becoming the "new normal," researchers have long been touting what Daniel Goleman called "the medical value of relationships" while warning of their absence.

> Studies done over two decades involving more
> than thirty-seven thousand people show that social
> isolation—the sense that you have nobody with whom
> you can share your private feelings or have close
> contact—doubles the chances of sickness or death.[3]

The power of social connections is, quite literally, life-giving.

Some readers will now think, *I have friends and a loving family, so I'm good, right?* For those blessed with true community, it is time to give thanks and not take such gifts for granted. But the journey out of lukewarminess leads us beyond the safe confines of our familiar relationships.

One of the most shocking (or sometimes soothing) things we can do is welcome someone because they are *not* in our circle of friends. Why crowd your life with the inconvenience of strangers? First, it has been my general observation that an unwelcoming attitude at the fringes of a relational world soon eats its way inward. Unfriendly habits cannot be contained at the edge of a life. Soon they will show up much closer to home. Second, the scriptural mandate to welcome others explicitly includes those who are not easy and comfortable friends.

> The journey out of lukewarminess leads us beyond the safe confines of our familiar relationships.

It is God's way, and now it is to be ours.

Made in the image of our triune God, we were hardwired for loving community. On this much we agree. But God generously offers his love and the chance for relationship. So, too, must we. When we settle for less, life on this planet—in tangible ways—dies off.

This must be why that little boy's words startled me and stirred a longing in my chest. I didn't need research findings to understand the importance of this, it was his sweet act of kindness that jolted me back to what I ached for and what the world desperately needs.

The next time it could be me welcoming someone.

It could be me turning to sense the nodding approval of my heavenly Father, who saw it all. But the truth is, something will need to change, for this is not always my first reaction. Not nearly enough, not yet. And while I sat and thought about those two words the rest of the flight, it will serve us well to now go further with a few more words.

Beyond the concept of welcoming, a powerful practice is called for.

THE LOST ART OF HOSPITALITY

It's more than an art, really: It's an ancient virtue with which we have almost lost touch. What follows in this section is barely the beginning of a conversation being conducted by many. Consider it an appetizer to awaken your hunger for something more.

In these fractious and fearful times, there may be no more important distinctive of the Christian life than hospitality. This expression of God's outrageous love has the potential to quench the thirst for justice and reconciliation like the coldest waters of Colossae. In some forms, it will soothe and comfort old wounds and tired souls like the hot springs of Hierapolis.

The rancorous political debate of today serves as a timely example. All sides seem to forget that a scorched earth strategy leaves all of us standing in ashes at the end. No matter who wins, we all lose something. We must do this differently. Even when (and because) we will passionately disagree.

Whether you run to a border and stand sheepishly with people you almost went to war with or you've decided to jump into the work of God, you will encounter people not like you. They may not like you either. Your interests are different, your ideas about global problems, national elections, and what's really happening in your community are very different. For obvious and not-so-obvious reasons, you are simply not alike. And right now, you may not even like each other.

The first inclination for many is to retreat into that fortress.

Is it possible that God's people can lead the way to a different way? Can we have genuine conversations—even debate—in the midst of very real (and sometimes messy) issues? Could we learn how to welcome others in this unwelcoming world?

Yes, it is possible, and it may be the most thirst-quenchingly cold or soothingly warm thing you do this year. It also happens to be thoroughly biblical and leads to something for which we all long.

PURSUING PEACE

Most election seasons, I eventually come back to the twenty-ninth chapter of Jeremiah. As always, context is the key to unlocking a powerful passage. In the book of Jeremiah is a letter he sent through diplomatic channels to people living very much in exile in Babylon. (This was the empire ruling over Israel before the Persians of Esther's story took over.) In this section we find familiar words and a favorite verse of many about the plans God has for you. But read the whole correspondence for its fullest effect.

This is a message for any who feel lost and disconnected from the time in which they live. For me, it is often a touchpoint at election time—no matter who wins or what issues rule the day. Hence (spoiler alert for a few of you), it will probably come up again some November weekend.

What does Jeremiah say to a nation torn apart and to people living far from the future they'd imagined? He tells them the truth: This season of exile will last longer than you'd hoped, but it will end. God has not forgotten you. But now, in the middle of your predicament:

> Plant gardens, and eat the food you grow there. Marry and have children . . . Pursue the peace and welfare of the city where I sent you into exile.[4]

Pray for Babylon—the land of your enemy—for if it enjoys peace, you will live in that peace too. Pursue the good for the place where you live, even if you're convinced the good guys aren't in charge. Where these first recipients of this letter lived was not their own choice. They were decidedly unhappy with their current situation and must have felt quite powerless. Jeremiah told them to never forget who's in charge and whose plan is unfolding. Never forget who is really in control.

In the meantime, keep pursuing and praying for peace.

It's a question worth asking: Do we pray for the shalom of the city in which we live? Or do we passively wait for others to make things better while we sit safely ensconced in our balconies? Remember, shalom is not only the absence of conflict but that blessed wholeness, the broken put back together. Do we actively pursue this for our communities?

> Shalom is not only the absence of conflict but that blessed wholeness, the broken put back together.

In such a divided world, peace seems but a dream. What does it look like to do more than pray for shalom? The choices are many, and the need is great. Remember that even small, good steps can lead to big chain reactions. Here's one you may have overlooked.

The practice of hospitality is a tangible pursuit of shalom. In these days of waning hope, could not this be our time to recapture and relearn this almost-forgotten practice?

First, we need to agree on what the word itself means, for it has lapsed into weaker uses.

A WORKING DEFINITION

Theologian Soong-Chan Rah warns about hospitality as a goal: "The church must decide what kind of hospitality it is willing to extend—traditional Western hospitality or *a more demanding, biblical form of hospitality.*" Are we willing, in other words, to come into "the fullness of what Christ originally intended"?[5]

Before we look at this more demanding, biblical form of hospitality, let's clear out some of those weaker uses. If hospitality conjures up images of napkins folded into the shape of animals and cucumber sandwiches served at high tea, hit the delete button in your brain right now. I know, for a minute it will be impossible to not think of those little napkin sculptures, but that is NOT the biblical concept of hospitality.

It's not even primarily the less formal backyard barbecue, though we should come back soon to the idea of eating together. It is not merely an event, though those will certainly flow out of its practice. Hospitality is a godly way of navigating this world full of people we mostly don't know (yet). It is an overarching value that colors how we interact with the vast majority of this planet's population with which we have less in common (at least at first). Author and professor Christine Pohl puts it like this in her book:

> If hospitality involves sharing your life and sharing in the lives of others, guests/strangers are not first defined by their need. Lives and resources are much more complexly intertwined, and roles are much less predictable.[6]

As we welcome others, expect the unexpected.

We soon find when exploring the Scriptures that the roles interchange throughout the narrative: God as host, Israel as guest, a family as host, God as guest, Jesus as guest and then host, early Christians the same. Throughout it all is that complex intertwining of lives and experiences—receiving one another into homes, families, and hearts.

Perhaps we're getting ahead of ourselves.

Hospitality is an ancient virtue found in nomadic cultures traveling in harsh and sometimes lifeless lands. The practice of welcoming another was not merely a way of life; on some days, it *was* life. To this day, many cultures throughout

Hospitality is a godly way of navigating this world full of people we mostly don't know (yet).

the world see the honoring of a guest as the highest of priorities. Far from home, I have found myself more than a little humbled at the manner with which I was received into a home or community. For me, each time is still a jolt. For my hosts, it comes as a surprise that I would be so surprised at their hospitality.

SURPRISING GUESTS

The story of Abraham is our most complete picture of this practice in the Old Testament. In Genesis 18, we find him near the great trees of Mamre, resting during the heat of the day, when three visitors appear. When the great patriarch saw them, "he hurried from the entrance of his tent to meet them and bowed low to the ground."[7] Keep reading, and you'll see him welcome them warmly—"here's water to freshen up while will I get you a morsel of bread before you're on your way."[8] That little something to eat turns out to be just-baked bread with butter and a calf that would be hurriedly cooked over the fire (okay, so barbecue is involved).

In his commentary on Genesis, Derek Kidner states that all the details surrounding this lavish meal, "are still characteristic of Bedouin hospitality, even to the host's insistence in some cases on standing . . . until his guests have finished."[9] To share food like this is to share your life with someone.

We are witnessing a gracious and intimate moment in this aged tale.

You might remember the rest of the story: those were no "ordinary" guests, but two angels accompanying the Lord himself, who had very important news for Abraham and Sarah. Henri Nouwen observes that Old and New Testament stories like these show the obligation to welcome the stranger, but then says these stories "tell us that guests are carrying precious gifts with them, which they are eager to reveal to a receptive host."[10]

Don't miss the point. Your guest is not defined only by their need. It could be your lack of something which shows up in this welcoming. This is where the lives and resources of guest and host intertwine. It is here that surprises make an appearance.

Pohl sums it up: "In the stories involving hospitality in the Old Testament, blessing is very frequently present."[11] Is it too much for us to anticipate these blessings moving in all directions for *both host and guest*?

By the time we get to the gospels, we see Jesus accepting offers of hospitality from friends and enemies alike and hosting the most intimate of suppers on the night of his betrayal. Blessings, no doubt, flying in all directions.

And then, with Zacchaeus, Jesus flips the protocol script and invites himself into the hospitality of a well-known sinner.

FLIPPING THE SCRIPT

A dreaded tax collector, and chief among them at that, Zacchaeus climbed the sung-about tree. Why? So he could see better. Little did he know how much better he would soon see. We know the story well: Jesus sees this curious sinner completely and then speaks the words that would change everything: "I must stay at your house today."

Jesus wanted more than a memorable encounter. "It's only proper I go to your house," is another way to render the text. "This must happen, Zacchaeus." Around the table flowed forgiveness, the financial repair of past harm and, to the murmuring crowd, the proclamation we still revere. This traitor turned penitent believer is *restored*, for Jesus declares: "today salvation has come to this house." For those watching who were still confused, Jesus plainly states that "the Son of Man came to seek and to save the lost."[12]

What blessing poured from the guest to the host that day. This is the heart and mission of Jesus. Go back one last time to Revelation 3:

Here I am! I stand at the door and knock. If anyone
hears my voice and opens the door, I will come in and eat
with that person, and they with me.[13]

This is the comingling of lives, the place of laughter and tears,
of stories and hopes. It is where vulnerability flourishes in safety.
These are the trappings of relationship.

It is what Jesus does.

It is what his followers are called to do.

In biblical forms of hospitality, a relationship emerges from
which blessings can flow in all directions. How, then, does this
apply to our broken world? How can this practice be an expression of our pursuit of shalom? How do we keep this from becoming an idealistic garden party—cucumber sandwiches included?
Most of us do not live as Bedouins, nor will we welcome the
incarnate God to a cookout. My assumption here is that few of
us have recently climbed a tree to see Jesus in person, much less
have him over for dinner. How then does the biblical view of
hospitality show up in our lives?

Some practical handles might help.

IT IS NOT AN OPTION

This practice is not only the responsibility of those to whom such
things come easily. This is beyond spiritual giftedness. To leave
the "welcoming" to such people is tantamount to leaving the sharing of our faith to "evangelists" or teaching to "teachers." Even
without certain giftings, we are each to share our faith personally,
yes? We will all teach others in this life. How strange and inept
the Christian life would be if we stood around and waited for
specialists to do every single thing for us.

At a more base level, this would be like saying we can pick
and choose which aspects of the Spirit-driven life we are more

comfortable with: *Self-control is not my thing; I'm more of a "joy" guy.* When Paul wrote Galatians 5:22, he did not present it as a smorgasbord. There are aspects of the Christian life that are not a matter of who is gifted to do what or what comes more naturally to some Christians than others.

From the clear and consistent call of Scripture, practicing hospitality is to be woven into the lives of each of us who have been welcomed home.

IT IS MORE THAN YOU THINK

This way of being in a world of strangers is stressed throughout the Scriptures. But now notice what is being said:

> Keep on loving one another as brothers and sisters. Do not forget to show hospitality to strangers.[14]

The words for "loving one another" and "showing hospitality to strangers" are stunning when put alongside each other.[15]

- Keep on loving one another (*philadelphia*)
- Do not forget to show hospitality (*philoxenia*)

You might recognize *philadelphia* as the word for loving your brother (or sister). But Christopher J. H. Wright says our translation of *philoxenia* is "too weak": "[It] literally means 'love of the stranger, the outsider.' It is the diametric opposite of xenophobia."[16]

Do not forget to love the stranger, the outsider. The admonition is clear and outrageous. It is more than you think.

IT MUST BE DELIBERATE

In the life that never settles for less than God's best, we keep encountering intentionality. It is no different here. As with previous steps we are taking, this will require a moment of decision. In the middle of Paul's call to loving action in Romans 12, we find this simple sentence:

Practice hospitality.[17]

In the original language, the word *practice* has more oomph to it. In other places, Paul uses the same word to describe "press[ing] on toward the goal."[18] This will require concerted effort. By God's grace, step toward this long-standing command and witness the extraordinary work of God—the creation of something not there before.

IT CREATES A SPACE FOR SOMETHING NEW TO EMERGE

In Nouwen's book devoted in part to hospitality, he offers an intriguing definition:

Hospitality, therefore, means primarily the creation of a free space where the stranger can enter and become a friend instead of an enemy.[19]

Strong words such as *friend* and *enemy* make us uncomfortable. "I don't see that stranger as my enemy per se, he (or she) is just not my friend." Fair enough. Given the "right" combination of "wrong" stances (be they political, theological, or practical), however, we soon find ourselves polarized. Now you're on the other side of the debate, and I want nothing to do with you or your kind.

Doesn't that start to sound like an enemy?

Seeing the practice of hospitality as another opportunity for God to create something new means beginning to acknowledge him in this process. Liken this space—this is me talking, not Nouwen—to a sanctuary of sorts where something (in this case, a relationship) can find rooting and slowly take life. At this point, it is but a patch of ground cleared, but soon, something new emerges.

Again, this will take some work.

IT WILL NOT COME NATURALLY
BUT SUPERNATURALLY

We no longer thrive in the garden of God's making. We live "east of Eden,"[20] where struggle and sin mar what he intended. It does not mean beauty is lost to the primordial past. It will simply require far more effort now. Is this not what God told Adam in that heartbreaking moment after the fall?

In our approach to hospitality we should expect to work. We might even break a sweat. Clearing out the weeds that choke out the potential for God's best will require energy and patience—and a ruthlessly realistic mindset.

This honest assessment of the situation begins with us. Nouwen suggests thinking about this as a continuum, with hostility on one end and hospitality on the other.

$$\longleftrightarrow$$

Hostility   Hospitality

Do not think of this as an "either/or" proposition. Imagine living in the tension of both realities—depending on your own scars, your current work load, your past history with that person or people group, and let's face it, the mood that just blew in—you and I will *slide along this continuum.*[21]

If we are to enjoy any growth in this area, it would do us well to confess and pray along the way as we openly admit where we are on this scale at any given moment.

It might well start with "the shocking confrontation with our hostile self."[22] To discern such a distasteful thing in our true selves, we start by asking a series of questions:

- Am I fearful? Why?
- Am I looking to straighten "them" out?
- Am I placing the failure of another on this person's shoulders?
- Am I doing this for the optics of me being "the nice Christian?"
- Am I willing to see something come to life between us?
- Am I willing for this to cost me something?

The questions are endless, the point is the same. Can we face the level of hostility we have about a person or group of people? There won't be much movement toward hospitality without this.

Interestingly, this does not mean an "absence" of hostility is required to see progress. It is the humble awareness of where we are on this scale that allows for growth.

IT ISN'T ABOUT ME

This has already become apparent but is worth stating aloud: Steps toward hospitality in the purest biblical sense cannot loop back to us. Not our glory. Not our agenda. We are making space for people to move from enemy to friend, not "their side" to "our side." I am now making room for someone who is, in many ways, a stranger, with all their eccentricities, viewpoints, and habits. Strange indeed.

What does it mean to create a space where I start to see you more and more as a fellow image-bearer of God? "[It] means inviting the stranger into our world on his or her terms."[23]

Perhaps nothing cuts against the narcissistic grain more than inviting someone into your world on their terms. This becomes an expression of servanthood, which is why it is so powerful. It involves a sacrifice, which is why it so difficult. This is also why Peter warns us to do this without complaining.[24] He anticipates our reaction to such a selfless move. Pay attention to the telltale grumbling, for with it comes a slide toward the hostile.

> Lorne Sanny, the [former president] of Navigators, was once asked how you could tell if you really were a servant. "By how you act," he said, "when you're treated like one."[25]

IT IS ABOUT LISTENING

In the aftermath of a hate-filled attack against people protesting a racially charged right-wing rally in Charlottesville, Virginia, in 2017, some struggled to fully hear the cries from African Americans all too familiar with this evil. Ann Voskamp posted a thought as eloquent and hauntingly convicting as anything I've read from her. It was an invitation to a different sort of listening that leads to a different kind of living:

> Listening not to defend and listening not to debate, but listening to deeply digest the experience and perspective and prayers of your brothers and sisters in Christ . . . [to] pick up our Cross, and live the cruciform life of the upside down Kingdom that brings shalom in the face of everything.[26]

This is a skill I will never fully master but must never stop pursuing: *Listen hard when it's hard to listen.*

Listen hard when it's hard to listen.

Do not interrupt even when it provides relief from what you're hearing. Keep listening. Keep asking curious and humble questions. And when there is nothing to say, dare to sit with someone in the quiet. There is much healing that begins to happen in active silence.

Eventually, when the silence breaks, better words will now have a better chance of being formed.

IT WILL EVENTUALLY BE TIME TO SPEAK

The receiving of someone into your life means they will learn about you as well.

The tapestry of your experiences, stories, loves, and fears should not be hidden. What you eat, listen to, read, and dream about must be on humble display in your home. How odd would it be if you or I were invited into a space only to be gawked at, probed, and observed? This sounds more like a laboratory than a garden. More like an experiment than dinner around a table. Instead, our words are shared and revealed in risky revelation to each other.

Risky, yes, for what if we say something the wrong way?

Pray for wisdom here, and do not fill the awkward spaces with even more awkward words. Proverbs beckons us to another practice we've misplaced in our instant-reply society: thinking before we speak. "Do you see someone who speaks in haste? There is more hope for a fool than for them."[27]

Taking the extra beat helps.

Still, there will always be words. True words are good. True words leavened with humility are better. True words leavened with humility and sprinkled with grace are best of all. This is when something new pushes up through the hardened soil of that patch of ground you cleared.

It is the beginning of real conversation. Small, safe, but no-less-real words are shared about the details of a life. Some will dismiss this as "small talk," but there is nothing small about sharing the laughs and sighs of our day. This is when our humanity shows up.

Those matters separating us will also make a tentative appearance. Frictions and fears do not vanish mysteriously. But we do understand them better alongside the frustrations of another who shares their heart. We still differ, but we are different than before. Less fragile, perhaps? And in that strength, more generous.

Too often, we expect the people we invite into our homes and lives to soften on a particular stance simply by spending time with us. This certainly happens, but it cannot be the goal. In my own limited experience in such things, it is often *my* heart which begins to soften.

That will be enough for now.

It is enough for you.

Soon, as believers, some of our next good words become prayers. Better prayers. Cries to God with each other and for each other. Now we have more in common than before. The "strangeness" becomes more familiar. And with it, our prayers take on new life.

IN THIS SPACE, WE'LL SEE A FAMILIAR MARK

In the story of Abraham's hospitality, we soon learn that his guests were anything but ordinary. Indeed. Most of us have not been witness to such theophanic goings-on as described in Genesis. The Lord of all showing up with two wingmen (pun intended)? Puh-leeze. Those guests that day were beyond the ordinary.

With careful disclaimers, our guests are also beyond ordinary themselves. Clearly, we are not gods, nor are our guests. We are not angels, nor are most of our guests—though the writer of Hebrews leaves that specific possibility dangling in our imaginations.[28] Even so, the people we host and make room for in our lives, hearts, and homes are anything but ordinary. In *The Weight of Glory*, C. S. Lewis said it outright:

> There are no *ordinary* people. You have never talked to a mere mortal . . . it is immortals whom we joke with, work with, marry, snub, and exploit.[29]

Lest we so soon forget, we each bear the image of the Most High God. Such thoughts should motivate us. As John Calvin observed:

Therefore, whatever man you meet who needs your aid, you have no reason to refuse to help him. Say, "He is a stranger"; but the Lord has given him a mark that ought to be familiar to you.[30]

This image of God is enough, he suggests, to recommend this stranger to you, making him (or her) "worthy of your giving yourself and all your possessions."[31]

When we recognize the mark that ought to be familiar, this ancient practice has already begun its work. It is worth our effort and the steep costs that come our way. Sliding on the continuum between hostility and hospitality, a healing emerges—of jaded fears and deepest hurts. It does not happen as quickly as we'd like, but it need not take as long as we fear.

The blessings fly in all directions. The role of host and guest begins to blur. It is a sight to behold, and the world could stand a whole lot more of this.

A SIGHT OF WHAT'S TO COME

One day, many will see what this looks like in unfettered glory. From Isaiah to Matthew to Revelation, a great feast is foretold: a meal resplendent with blessings overflowing. A time of celebration. Also a gathering of people from every tribe, tongue, and nation spanning time, culture, and opinions of the day. Then we will see in full what we can only catch in glimpses today.

And yes, food and drink appear at this feast. This would not be the time to put too fine a detail on this thought, for "now I know in part; then I shall know fully."[32] I will, however, mention that I take great encouragement from Jesus eating food in his resurrected body.

For now, allow all those shared meals throughout the timeline of Scripture to compel us to specific acts of grace in our time. Biblical hospitality is not a never-ending series of potluck dinners chained together by guilt-tinged obligation. It is the start of something new and the taste of something more. Around cups and plates and tables large and small, we have occasion to watch God create in this space between us.

His power shows up around that table.

Margaret Feinberg writes of a pattern running through all such meals: "God had been intentional in each gathering. He used these encounters to uncover a deep need and satiate a deep hunger."[33] Yes. Please, God. Do this. My heart yearns for this as my stomach growls for such a thing.

Of course, measured steps will now be taken in a world unsure about close connection. Legitimate short-term cautions will unfortunately line up next to our longer list of excuses, and before long, we will be lured back to the same old lukewarm ways.

Now more than ever, we cannot settle.

I do not know your next step, but there must be one. Take it, and see what happens. What if in the most unlikely of times, the people of God started a movement, a revolution of biblical hospitality? We are, after all, on this flight together.

As permissible (and it will be), invite strangers onto your row. Listen to their stories and watch their strangeness fade. Keep blessing them. Walk around the cabin. When the time is right, by all means, eat together. Change seats, and sit near someone who does not see things as you do. Now look again, and notice they, too, have gifts and blessings to bring.

Remember: This will not always go as planned. Expect some turbulence ahead. But let us vow on this day to settle no longer for the hateful, fearful way. The time has come for us to be wonderfully, shockingly different.

Welcome aboard.

FOR PERSONAL REFLECTION

- When was the last time you experienced radical hospitality? How did it bless you?
- What holds you back from welcoming others and inviting them into your life?

EPILOGUE

Music of the Dawn

ONE NIGHT IN MANAGUA, Nicaragua, it was my honor to stay in the home of a very generous family in an extremely impoverished part of the city. I was humbled by their hospitality as this family, like the rest of their church, welcomed a few of us doing some work in their city. The meal my hosts gave me, black beans and warm tortillas, probably cost them more than any meal I've ever served to a guest.

Like I said, I was humbled to the core.

Now it was time to get some sleep before an early flight home. As it turns out, I was sharing my room with a man I did not know from another US church. We were shown to a couple of cots in a fairly narrow room at the back of their home, with mudbrick walls and a makeshift tin roof overhead. A torn curtain served as a makeshift door.

I set my alarm and hoped the charge in my phone would last. Placing my backpack on the floor, I started getting ready for bed.

Cue the first sound of the evening.

My roommate must have worked especially hard that day, for as soon as he collapsed on his cot, he slid almost immediately into a deep and unhindered rest that allowed him to snore freely and fully.

It was impressive, that sound. I was in for a long night.

I pulled the string on the bare bulb hanging in our room, bringing the dark. Lying there, I tried my best to ignore what now sounded like a barrel full of chainsaws. But wait, what's that—another sound? Clicking and crunching. Odd. My ears began to dial in the location of this strange noise and I realized it wasn't coming from his direction, but rather from the wall right next to my cot. I used my phone to shine a light on the wall to see what all the noise was about.

Not a good idea.

The wall had come to life with insects of every variety you can imagine crawling in and out of the holes and crevasses in the mud bricks. A movie came to mind from the dusty archives of antiquity (or, as I like to call them, "the 80s"). For those too young to remember, *Indiana Jones and the Temple of Doom* contains a scene which makes the skin crawl from a wall covered with innumerable bugs.

I thought such things only happened in the movies.

A wall trembling with the activity of a thousand creepy crawlies right next to me. That's how my night began: *Texas Chainsaw* on my right and a nightmare to my left. Ladies and Gentlemen, I give you Insomnia Symphony no. 1.

I didn't have any earplugs, so I tore pages from my journal to stick in my ears. I had two goals: (1) to muffle the sound as best I could; and (2) to keep things from crawling into my head.

Having done all I could think to do, I started praying. Not even for sleep—I was praying for the dawn.

Later that night I was awakened from my restless sleep by the third sound of the evening. Something had entered our makeshift room and was scrounging and snooping underneath my bed. And then it was gone.

In the dark, I couldn't place the weight and rhythm of the steps padding down the dirt hallway. This was certainly not a cat or dog or even a pig. *Please, Lord, don't let it be a three-pound insect.* Before long I heard the sound again, and with the light of my iPhone, I caught a glimpse of what had awakened me.

A couple of roosters.

What a relief! Yes, yes, because roosters are less disturbing to me than five-inch millipedes and all their crawly friends. But there was another reason: *If these fellas are moving around,* I began to think, *then morning can't be far away.*

Sure, it was still dark. At first glance, all the evidence pointed to a night still in full swing. The other sounds in my room were certainly still going strong. And yet, the sound of roosters stirred up a hope in my slightly freaked-out heart.

Sure enough, it was not long before I heard the fourth and most glorious sound of the night—the one I'd been waiting and praying for all night long. The roosters eventually started crowing at the sky.

I couldn't have been more thrilled. Why? You already know that answer: They were announcing the dawn. The long, creepy, restless night was over. The morning would now take over.

I took great comfort in that glorious sound.

THE SOUNDS OF OUR SOUNDTRACK

What's the most comforting sound you can imagine?

Though yours may differ from mine, here's what our favorite sounds have in common: They quickly stir up powerful emotions. Auditory neuroscientist Seth Horowitz tells us that from nineteenth-century psychology to twenty-first-century neural imaging, sound is consistently found to be "one of the most important and fastest-acting triggers for emotion."[1] Sound gives us context and warnings and clues to our world. Elsewhere Horowitz states, "Everything you hear has some kind of an impact on you and changes how you respond to the rest of the world."[2] Though it's often in the background, sound is the basis for many "very complex cognitive responses."[3]

Hmmm. (That was the sound of me thinking).

These days the sounds in our world are mostly loud and angry and anything but comforting. Disconcerting? Scary? Infuriating? Exhausting? Discouraging? No wonder some are tempted to blend in rather than stand out, hold back rather than move forward. The sounds that affect our responses to this world are overwhelmingly negative and more than a little intimidating.

If the noise gets loud enough, we might just choose to settle.

So, in the closing pages, am I suggesting to plug your ears to keep from being discouraged? Is the last travel tip for your journey out of lukewarminess to bring earplugs? Try not to get too distracted with all the negativity flying through the air? Such an approach is not the answer; instead, it's akin to *not seeing* the full truth of what is happening all around us.

In whatever form, denying the truth is never the answer.

There is, of course, an importance to protecting which sounds we take in, for this God-given sense of hearing is always on. As Julian Treasure reminds us in one of his TED talks,[4] we have no earlids.

Long before the findings of neuroscience, the writers of Scripture offered commonsense wisdom about such matters. From the Psalmist's warning against walking in the "counsel of the wicked"[5] to Paul's against "hollow and deceptive philosophy,"[6] the point is well made: Pay attention to the soundtrack of your everyday life. Even the background noise has an effect. How about that? The simple song of many a childhood got it right:

Be careful, little ears, what you hear . . .

LISTENING FOR OTHER SOUNDS

Again, being careful does not mean we stop listening. A life that is soothingly hot AND thirst-quenchingly cold will not ignore the very real sounds of a world in distress. Let's return to a Scripture referenced in that same opening section of the book:

> We know that the whole creation has been groaning as in the pains of childbirth right up to the present time.[7]

The immediate context of this passage is the suffering of living in our not-yet-restored home. If you keep reading, Paul tells us it's not just the planet which groans—so, too, do we.

That vivid description of life rings true every time I hear it. But thankfully, Romans 8 speaks also of a future glory that awaits us. As much as I appreciate the honesty about the present, I'm desperate to hear the promise of our future.

This is a key to our survival in new and unfamiliar territory.

We who follow Jesus into the world and now vow to live differently had best be listening for other sounds amidst the noise. Sounds that bring life. Sounds that stir up strong feelings of resolve and love, of course. But also, like never before, hope. The sounds and stories of hopelessness grow louder by the day. Such groans are real and must not be ignored. We need, however, other stories and stronger truths in our ears. In short, we need hope ringing in our ears.

We need hope ringing in our ears.

Otherwise, we end up responding to the rest of the world like the rest of the world.

THE EDGE OF MORNING

Some are tempted to think the morning will never come. This explains much of what we hear from the rest of the world. Death still finds us, tragedy still wounds, and the acts of the unjust still leave their mark. We live in a groaning world where the shadows still cling to the night.

But because of the Resurrection, hope shimmers in those shadows. The darkness lingers, but morning is inevitable. In the words of N. T. Wright:

> The sun has begun to rise. Christians are called to leave behind, in the tomb of Jesus Christ, all that belongs to the brokenness and incompleteness of the present world. . . . That, quite simply, is what it means to be Christian: to follow Jesus Christ into the new world, God's new world, which he has thrown open before us.[8]

That's it—the sun has begun to rise. We do not fully see it, but we live on the edge of morning.

Listen carefully: There are roosters in the hallway.

HEARING IS EASY, LISTENING IS NOT

Unless you've experienced some genetic, developmental, or environmental complication, hearing is quite natural. As Horowitz observes, vertebrates have been doing it for a very long time. But then this:

> Listening, really listening, is hard when potential distractions are leaping into your ears every fifty-thousandth of a second—and pathways in your brain are just waiting to interrupt your focus.[9]

As you break camp and move from the land of the safe and predictable, there will be many distractions "leaping into your ears." They will distract you and demand your attention. They will also drive your emotions—for better or worse. Toward life or death.

This is why we must listen for sounds that stir up resolve. Train yourself to pick out such things among the cacophony. They are surely there, though noticing them will require effort:

The laughter of a little one is more than cute—it reminds us of the pure joy for which we were made.

The voice of a friend is more than familiar—it speaks to relationship, which can stretch into forever.

The sigh of relief is often more than respite—it suggests the safety of another's presence.

The beauty of birdsong and the murmur of soft water are more than calming—they hint of Eden past and the promise of the new creation.

> We do not fully see it, but we live on the edge of morning.

We can learn to listen for hope in the moment. But in the constant static of voices and opinions, it's okay to plan ahead. It's essential, actually. We need all the help we can get.

A PLAYLIST FOR THE TRIP

At the close of this book comes the beginning of your journey into new territory—and with it, a few tried and true ways to keep hope ringing in your ears. Yes, these are "golden oldies," but for many, they are more overlooked than overplayed. As you leave the lukewarm and, in many ways, re-engage the world around you, set yourself up for success by folding these practices into your life:

- *Let the sound of Scripture find its way to your ears.* Psalm 19 tells us that the words of Scripture refresh the soul, make wise the simple, give joy to the heart and light to the eyes. Who doesn't want that? Listen to Scripture being read out loud, taught by others, prayed, and confessed to one another in the regular, embodied rhythms of your week.

- *Let the words of a friend land in your heart.* "You're not crazy for caring that much" or "I'll go with you" are more life-giving than some of us are willing to admit. When strong words come your way, don't deflect them with pseudohumility. Wait a beat before responding, and allow those comments to find their mark.

- *Let the prayers of another echo long after the "Amen."* Listen to the voice of another praying for you—the tone, the care, the impassioned request made before God. There is a musicality to prayers that we seldom notice. Soak it in when that prayer has your name on it. Remember how God is hearing this prayer. And then, after it's over and you are alone, replay the beauty of those words.

- *Let the praises of God's people flood your hearing.* We often focus on the obvious vertical nature of worship, as we should. Colossians 3:16 also speaks about the horizontal effect such songs can have. Michael Horton aptly reminds us, "worship songs are intended not merely to facilitate personal expression of one's feelings but to sing the truth deeply into our hearts."[10] Oftentimes the sound of hope cuts through my noisy thoughts when I hear worship falling not just from my mouth but also from those gathered around me. These songs reverberate in my memory, and the truth soon finds its way into the deeper parts of me that need it most.

These "classics" never lose their effectiveness. Listen to them, alongside some of your personal favorites, to keep hope in your ears. Consider it your playlist for the journey forward.

THE MOST POWERFUL AND PERSONAL SOUND

We head into this uncharted land together, for together is how we were sent by our Savior. Anything less and we've settled for less.

But there is a powerful sound so personal and private, it is not audible on most days, if ever. It is the reminder that we are, by God's grace, his beloved.

The Spirit himself testifies with our spirit that we are God's children.[11]

Image-bearers of the Almighty who have turned to Jesus now have the same Holy Spirit that raised Jesus from the dead so close and available to us that the best way for the apostle Paul to explain it was to say things like "God's Spirit dwells in you."[12] This is exactly what Jesus promised.[13]

When the Spirit of God mysteriously whispers or seemingly shouts that we are Abba's children, he is breathing life into our tattered souls and courage into our despair. This, too, is the sound of hope as we follow Jesus into this world.

You are a new creation, and you will not go alone.

There is more to you than you know.

In this shadow-filled world, there are roosters announcing the light of morning. The night will not last, and the triumph of our good God is assured. Until that glorious day, never lose hope, you children of the dawn. Until Jesus returns, never settle, you sons and daughters of the King.

Make a choice to make a difference, and then behold the power of God in a thousand times a thousand chain reactions rippling through eternity for his glory.

> You are a new creation, and you will not go alone. *There is more to you than you know.*

FOR PERSONAL REFLECTION

- What does the soundtrack of hope sound like to you? What words and prayers do you need to hear more often?
- How often do you speak comforting words into someone else's life? In what ways can you be better at pushing against the noise of our world?

ACKNOWLEDGMENTS

SEVERAL PAGES AGO, I challenged you to not just count your blessings but name them.

Now it's my turn.

There are many who made this book possible. Each of them is a blessing. I wish there were space to name them all, but alas, the pages are now few till the end. Suffice it to say, "There were others."

First, thank you to my publisher, Don Pape. Your continued faith in me, coupled with encouragement, is a gift to this not-always-secure writer. Thanks also to David Zimmerman, my editor, who braves the virtual white water of my thoughts and stories and turns the raft back when I've drifted too far. Thanks also to the rest of the team at NavPress and Tyndale—to Elizabeth Schroll for her keen eye and generous help in the copyediting, to Eva Winters for a cover design that sums up the hot and the cold of it, and to Robin Bermel and her team for dreaming big with us. And thanks to my agent, Mark Sweeney, for his help in this process.

To the leadership team at The Crossing: Thank you for navigating the uncharted waters of our VUCA world with such integrity. To Randall, Andy, Anthony, Tim, Rob, Joel, and the rest of our pastors: Thank you for running to borders and into the fray as brokers of shalom.

To the people of The Crossing: Your passion and generosity is a sight to behold. I can't wait to see what God has in store for us in the coming days. You were made for such a time as this.

To others who have stretched my thinking and clarified my writing: Steve, your letters are a bracing blast of truth. Ben, thanks for helping me get the details right. Matt, your love of the Scriptures is contagious. Dale, thanks for reading the manuscript with an editor's eye and a pastor's heart. Lisa, the power of your wisdom often comes in the gentlest of words, and I am so grateful God brought you into my life.

To Donna: Your care for me and my family is hard to describe but impossible to ignore. What a gift you are to Robin and me.

To the many friends who have never once resembled a grumpy Muppet in some remote balcony: You've jumped into the story and on the grand stage, and I can't imagine doing any of this without you. To the men who laughed and squirmed their way in and out of a cave in Nepal: Thanks for an adventure we'll never forget. To Steve and Amanda and the world you keep inviting me into. To Mike for allowing me to partner with you in championing churches in Africa, India, and beyond. To the Le Montrachet group: Thanks for letting me read a chapter about hobbits and refugees, and for encouraging me the way you did.

To Rick and Kristi: Thank you for sticking with our fledgling church all those years ago. That one choice started a chain reaction for the Kingdom you can't yet imagine. To Steve and Judy: I'm forever grateful God led you from Philly to our cul-de-sac. Oh, the plans of our sovereign God and the stories we will tell for all eternity. For John, Wiley, and Dave: I'm so grateful for your constant care of me.

To our moms, Jackie and Ann: You've shown our families how to love and live beyond the grief. And thanks to that loving family with whom I can laugh and cry and hope and cheer for that *blessed assurance* that is ours.

To Michael and Jeremy: Thank you for loving my daughters well and tolerating an oft-repeated story or two. May there be more that include us all.

To my extraordinary daughters, Alex and Tori: My mind drifts back to those glorious days when together we'd read of the great king Aslan. Thank you for giggling at funny voices and asking great questions. Alex, perhaps the day will soon come when I might introduce your Kennedy to the great king.

Tori: Your work on this book (and so much more God is doing in our midst) is almost beyond words. You are so clearly following God's call, and it is my great privilege to watch it happen.

To Robin: All the adventures, triumphs, and surprises pale in comparison to the day I met you under that magnolia tree in front of Alexander Hall. That God allowed my story to intertwine yours is one of the great plot twists of my life. Thank you, my love, for never settling for anything less than God's best in our family, our ministry, and our life together.

Wow. The experts were right. This gratitude business is good for the soul.

QUESTIONS FOR GROUP DISCUSSION

THROUGHOUT THIS BOOK, you'll encounter specific steps that lead the way out of lukewarminess. There are others, to be sure, that God will lead you to take along the way. The point of these questions is rather straightforward: This journey is not one to be taken alone. Surround yourself with at least a few people with whom you can share openly and dream mightily.

We head into this uncharted land together, for together is how we were sent by our Savior. Anything less and we've settled for less.

These discussion questions, coupled with the questions for personal reflection at the end of each chapter, are designed to help guide groups walking and living through *Never Settle*. Use these as jumping-off points, but stay alert to what God might be pointing out along the way to each of you.

And then, of course, this: Pray. Pray when you gather together. Pray when you're feeling stuck. Pray when you enter a new way of doing things and the uncertainty hints at fear. Pray when you start to wonder if such things are even worth it.

And pray for each other by name in front of each other.

Remember the God of heaven is leaning in and listening to every word. More than any other, he will go with you into this new land.

PROLOGUE

1. Why is it so common for people to settle in our world today?
2. What excites you about living the never-settled life?
3. What obstacles do you have to overcome to live the never-settled life?
4. When you feel stuck or settled, do you have anyone you confide in? Why or why not?
5. Share a prayer request you have for this upcoming week.

CHAPTER 1

1. What does it look like when Christians live lukewarm lives?
2. Have you ever felt like your faith was lukewarm? What did you do in those moments?
3. In what ways can your actions be shockingly refreshing, like the cold water of Colossae? And soothing, like the hot water of Hierapolis?
4. What is one step you can take this week to avoid lukewarminess?

CHAPTER 2

1. Describe a time you experienced one small, faithful act that made a big difference.
2. How is God uniquely calling you to make a difference in the world?
3. How have you seen "the myth of progress" fail?
4. What does it mean for you that God created you in his image?

5. What practical steps can you take to bless people (other image-bearers) whom God has placed in your life?

CHAPTER 3

1. In what ways have you encountered VUCA (volatility, uncertainty, complexity, ambiguity) in our world?
2. Practically, what does it look like to resist the patterns of this world and cling to hope?
3. What's one way you can incorporate reading Scripture into your life more regularly?
4. How does a biblical worldview change the way you view your current circumstances?
5. What would it look like for you to step into a community and process your doubts and struggles with other Christians? Do you already have a group like this? If not, pray for God to bring those people into your life.

CHAPTER 4

1. When have you felt like the prophet Elisha?
2. What does it look like to live in the world with spiritual blindness? Have you ever felt this way?
3. When has the enemy used your circumstances to pull your attention away from Jesus?
4. Why does self-awareness matter in our walk with God?
5. As you face life's challenges, how do you keep your eyes on Jesus, the champion who is for you?
6. Like Elisha, take some time to pray, asking God to awaken your soul and open your eyes to all the ways he is working in your life.

CHAPTER 5

1. What decisions do you find yourself making to "take back" your life from God?

2. Has pride ever made you feel "above God's help"?

3. In what areas of your life do you need to repent? What practical actions can you take in those areas?

4. We see that some "habits drift slowly and subtly back to lukewarm waters." What habits in your life do you need to adjust or leave behind?

5. How is God leading you out of Laodicea into the never-settled life?

CHAPTER 6

1. Do you believe that the small actions of one person can make a difference in the world? Why or why not?

2. Where do you need resilient faith to trust Jesus in your current circumstances?

3. What step is God calling you to take to start a chain reaction?

4. What are the great things that God has done in your past? How can you focus on them and remember that he'll be faithful in the present and the future?

5. Do you believe that God can use your one, faithful life to impact the Kingdom? Why or why not?

CHAPTER 7

1. What divisions do you see in the world today?

2. In your own life, where do you long for the peace—the shalom—of God?

3. In what ways can you pursue peacemaking and work to bring shalom in your everyday life?

4. Share a time when you have made a quick assumption about someone else instead of "run[ning] to the border" to get clarity.

5. Why is asking curious and humble questions an essential part of peacemaking?

6. How can you, like Phineas, lead the people in your life toward reconciliation? Be specific.

CHAPTER 8

1. In your own words, what is resilience?
2. How can you live an "antifragile" life in this world?
3. What steps can you take to practice humility in the midst of hardship?
4. Why are resilience, vulnerability, and humility important parts of the spiritual journey? Out of these three, which one do you struggle with the most?
5. What anxieties or worries do you need to bring before God and cast onto him? Take time to pray over the people in your group.

CHAPTER 9

1. When have you felt helpless? What did it look like for you to wait on God in those moments?
2. What are the differences between active and passive waiting?
3. What areas of your life do you need to surrender to Jesus in prayer?
4. Name three blessings in your life. Be specific.
5. How can the discipline of naming your blessings become a regular rhythm of your day?
6. This week, how can you braid your life together with God's?

CHAPTER 10

1. In what areas of your life do you act like a Muppet in the balcony? What cynical thoughts do you have about our world?

2. What makes slacktivism attractive? When have you acted like a "slacktivist?"
3. What echo chambers have you found yourself stuck in?
4. As part of God's handiwork, how has he uniquely gifted you? What injustice in the world is he calling you to address?
5. What fears do you have about stepping into the work that God is calling you to do?

CHAPTER 11

1. What does it look like for you to receive new people in the same way that Christ received you?
2. Why are relationships a vital part of living the never-settled life?
3. Where do you find yourself on the spectrum between hostility and hospitality?
4. What lessons about biblical hospitality from this chapter resonated with you? In what ways have they challenged you?
5. Who are the people you struggle to show hospitality to? Pray, asking Jesus to change your heart to see these people as fellow image-bearers.
6. What specific steps can you take to pursue shalom, practice hospitality, listen well, and bless others in the weeks to come?

EPILOGUE

1. Where has God challenged you as you've been reading *Never Settle*?
2. Think about the people you surround yourself with (in person and online). How consistently are their words and actions shockingly cold and soothingly hot?

3. Living the never-settled life requires community. Who in your life needs to join you on this journey?
4. What's been your biggest takeaway from *Never Settle*?
5. How will you make sure you don't slip back into lukewarm waters?
6. End your time together in prayer. Share where you've seen God at work and where you're longing for him to reveal himself. Remind each other of the life that God is calling each of you to.

NOTES

PROLOGUE: CHOICES, CHAIN REACTIONS & THE WAY OUT
1. *Translating the Great Commission*, a Barna Research report produced in partnership with Seed Company, barna.com/greatcommission/.
2. Matthew 28:19.
3. Matthew 28:20.
4. Genesis 1:1.
5. Genesis 1:31.
6. Genesis 17.
7. Matthew 28:20.
8. C. S. Lewis, *Mere Christianity* (San Francisco: HarperCollins, 2001), 92.
9. 1 Corinthians 13:1-3.

CHAPTER 1: WHAT MAKES JESUS PUKE
1. Revelation 1:14-18.
2. Revelation 3:15-16.
3. Quoted in E. Randolph Richards and Brandon J. O'Brien, *Misreading Scripture with Western Eyes: Removing Cultural Blinders to Better Understand the Bible* (Downers Grove, IL: IVP Books, 2012), 11.
4. Richards and O'Brien, *Misreading Scripture*, 11.
5. Revelation 3:20.

CHAPTER 2: HOBBITS, REFUGEES & THE *IMAGO DEI*
1. Greg Holder, *The Genius of One: God's Answer for Our Fractured World* (Colorado Springs: NavPress, 2017).
2. N. T. Wright, *Surprised by Hope: Rethinking Heaven, the Resurrection, and the Mission of the Church* (New York: HarperOne, 2008), 82.

3. Ken Gire, *Windows of the Soul: Hearing God in the Everyday Moments of Your Life* (Grand Rapids, MI: Zondervan, 1996), 48. The connections Gire makes between *The Hobbit* and the Christian life have been a significant influence on my thinking.

4. Gire, *Windows*, 48.

5. J. R. R. Tolkien, *The Hobbit* (New York: Houghton Mifflin Harcourt, 2012), chap. 1.

6. Genesis 1:1.

7. Robert E. Longacre, "Weqatal Forms in Biblical Hebrew Prose," in *Biblical Hebrew and Discourse Linguistics*, ed. Robert D. Bergen (Winona Lake, IN: Eisenbrauns, 1994), 50–98.

8. Thanks to Matt Lybarger, pastor at The Crossing, for sharing this wonderful insight with me in a conversation about Genesis.

9. Whitney Houston, "I Will Always Love You," *The Bodyguard: Original Soundtrack Album* © 1992 Arista. This song was written by Dolly Parton but Houston's cover of it is iconic.

10. E. Randolph Richards and Brandon J. O'Brien, *Misreading Scripture with Western Eyes: Removing Cultural Blinders to Better Understand the Bible* (Downers Grove, IL: IVP Books, 2012), 12.

11. Genesis 2:15. The Hebrew word used here is *shamar*.

12. Genesis 3:24 is the next usage of *shamar*. Here, it refers to the cherubim guarding the Tree of Life from the outcasts from Eden, Adam and Eve. For more information on *shamar*, see F. Brown, S. Driver, and C. Briggs, *The Brown-Driver-Briggs Hebrew and English Lexicon* (Peabody, MA: Hendrickson, 2005), 1036–37.

13. The name for God used in Genesis 1:1 (in the Hebrew Bible).

14. Gire, *Windows*, 49.

CHAPTER 3: LIVING IN A VUCA WORLD

1. "The Origins of VUCA," *Executive Development Blog*, UNC Kenan-Flagler Business School, March 10, 2017, http://execdev.kenan-flagler.unc.edu/blog/the-origins-of-vuca.

2. Romans 12:2.

3. Barna, "Competing Worldviews Influence Today's Christians," May 9, 2017, https://www.barna.com/research/competing-worldviews -influence-todays-christians/.

4. Barna includes foundational tenets such as the existence of absolute moral truth, the Bible's accuracy, the existence of Satan, and the reality of Jesus' sinless life (to name a few) in the definition of "biblical worldview." In other words, they take the basic beliefs of Christianity into account when surveying; https://www.barna.com/research/barna

-survey-examines-changes-in-worldview-among-christians-over-the
-past-13-years/.

5. Ravi Zacharias, *The Logic of God: 52 Christian Essentials for the Heart and Mind* (Grand Rapids, MI: Zondervan, 2019), 140.

6. Zacharias, *The Logic of God*, 141.

7. My thanks to a dear friend, Dan Allender, whose use of this term is important enough for each of us to pursue further. See his *To Be Told: God Invites You to Coauthor Your Future* (Colorado Springs: Waterbrook, 2006), 49–52.

8. Timothy George and Robert Smith, eds., *A Mighty Long Journey: Reflections on Racial Reconciliation* (Nashville: Broadman & Holman, 2000).

9. Robert Smith Jr., "The Big Idea: Preach in Light of the Eschaton," interview by Matt Woodley, PreachingToday.com, n.d., https://www.preachingtoday.com/skills/themes/big-idea/big-idea-preach-in-light-of-eschaton.html.

10. Robert Smith Jr., "The Big Idea: Preach in Light of the Eschaton," interview by Matt Woodley, PreachingToday.com.

11. In one of the ongoing discussions The Crossing pastors have in front of our congregation on weekends, Ben Horseman made this brilliant point about following Jesus.

12. John Stonestreet and Brett Kunkle, *A Practical Guide to Culture: Helping the Next Generation Navigate Today's World* (Colorado Springs: David C. Cook, 2020), 55–56.

13. C. S. Lewis, *The Lion, the Witch and the Wardrobe* (New York: Collier Books, 1979), 159–60.

CHAPTER 4: THE REAL BAT CAVE

1. John Newton, "Amazing Grace," 1772.

2. 2 Kings 6:10.

3. Slighted edited version of the lyrics "Every move you make, every step you take, I'll be watching you" from The Police, "Every Breath You Take," *Synchronicity* © 1983 A&M Records.

4. 2 Kings 6:12.

5. 2 Kings 6:17.

6. Isaiah 42:19-20.

7. Matthew 23:16-26.

8. Os Guinness, *The Call: Finding and Fulfilling God's Purpose for Your Life* (Nashville: W Publishing Group, 2018), 205.

9. Guinness, *The Call*, 205.

10. Ephesians 6:12.

11. John 16:33.

12. Paraphrasing C. S. Lewis, *The Screwtape Letters* (San Francisco: HarperOne, 2015), introduction.
13. Timothy Keller, "Sight for the Blind," sermon at Redeemer Presbyterian, New York, August 30, 2015. I am indebted to Keller throughout this chapter for his insights on this passage.
14. Isaiah 6:5, ESV.
15. Curt Thompson, *The Soul of Shame: Retelling the Stories We Believe about Ourselves* (Downers Grove, IL: IVP Books, 2015), 144.
16. John 8:44.
17. F. Brown, S. Driver, and C. Briggs, *The Brown-Driver-Briggs Hebrew and English Lexicon* (Peabody, MA: Hendrickson, 2005), 966. For a detailed account of Satan as the accuser see Walter Bauer, *A Greek-English Lexicon of the New Testament and Other Early Christian Literature*, revised and edited by Frederick William Danker (Chicago: University of Chicago Press, 1979), 916–17.
18. Thompson, *Soul of Shame*, 144.
19. Isaiah 6:7.
20. Isaiah 6:8, NET.
21. 2 Kings 6:16.
22. Adam Cole, "Colors," Radiolab, May 21, 2012, https://www.wnycstudios.org/podcasts/radiolab/episodes/211119-colors.
23. Ed Yong, "The Mantis Shrimp Sees Like a Satellite," January 23, 2014, https://www.nationalgeographic.com/science/phenomena/2014/01/23/the-mantis-shrimp-sees-like-a-satellite/.
24. 1 Corinthians 2:9, ESV.
25. 1 Corinthians 13:12.

CHAPTER 5: CHOOSE YOU THIS DAY

1. Francis A. Schaeffer, *Joshua and the Flow of Biblical History* (Wheaton, IL: Crossway, 2004), 221, quoted in *Expository Notes of Dr Thomas Constable*, CD-ROM, Sonic Light, 2001.
2. Joshua 24:15.
3. Turkish Archaeological News, "Laodicea on the Lycus," March 9, 2017, https://turkisharchaeonews.net/site/laodicea-lycus.
4. Daniel L. Akin, *Christ-Centered Exposition Commentary: Exalting Jesus in Revelation* (Nashville: Holman Reference, 2016), 101.
5. Simon Sinek, "Sometimes YOU are the PROBLEM!," January 3, 2018, https://www.vexplode.com/en/motivational/sometimes-you-are-the-problem-simon-sinek-simonsinek-entspresso-2/. Other tellings of this story have the details different.
6. Simon Sinek, "Sometimes YOU are the PROBLEM!," January 3, 2018.
7. James Hibberd, "*Westworld* Co-Creator Defends Complex Plotting,

Humanity Criticism," *Entertainment Weekly*, June 25, 2018, https://ew.com/tv/2018/06/25/westworld-interview-nolan/.

8. Romans 7:18, ESV.

9. N. T. Wright, *Surprised by Hope: Rethinking Heaven, the Resurrection, and the Mission of the Church* (New York: HarperOne, 2008), 87.

10. Francis Schaeffer, as quoted in Russ Greg, "Imago Dei Education: Bearing the Burden of My Neighbor's Glory" in *The Journal: A Conversation on Education in the Classical Tradition*, no. X (Fall 2017): 14, accessed February 25, 2020, https://societyforclassicallearning.org/wp-content/uploads/2017/12/SCL-Journal-Fall-2017-digital.pdf.

11. Wright, *Surprised by Hope*, 87.

12. Romans 8:37.

13. Revelation 1:12-18.

14. Romans 8:11.

15. Psalm 46:1.

16. Admiral William McRaven, commencement speech, University of Texas at Austin, May 17, 2014, http://alcalde.texasexes.org/2014/05/mcraven-to-grads-to-change-the-world-start-by-making-your-bed/.

17. Revelation 3:19.

18. Lecrae Moore, with Jonathan Merritt, *Unashamed* (Nashville: B&H Publishing Group, 2016), 59.

19. Revelation 3:20.

20. Daniel L. Akin, *Exalting Jesus in Revelation*, Christ-Centered Exposition Commentary (Nashville: Holman Reference, 2016), 108.

21. Patrologia Graeca 91:1057d, as quoted in Robert Louis Wilken, *The Spirit of Early Christian Thought* (New Haven, CT: Yale University Press, 2003), 131.

CHAPTER 6: CHAIN REACTION

1. 1 Thessalonians 5:18.

2. Fuller Youth Institute, "Can I Ask That?," vimeo clip, accessed January 23, 2020, https://fulleryouthinstitute.org/askthat.

3. Fanny Crosby, "Blessed Assurance," 1873.

4. Hebrews 11:32, 35.

5. Acts 22:22-23.

6. Acts 23:10.

7. Acts 23:16.

8. W. J. Conybeare and J. S. Howson, *The Life and Epistles of St. Paul* (Grand Rapids, MI: Eerdmans, 1987), 721.

9. Philippians 1:13.

10. Philippians 1:14.

11. Rodney Stark, *The Rise of Christianity: A Sociologist Reconsiders History* (Princeton, NJ: Princeton University Press, 1996), 6.
12. Philippians 4:22, emphasis added.
13. Justo L. González, *The Story of Christianity*, vol. 1: The Early Church to the Dawn of the Reformation (San Francisco: HarperOne, 2010), 35.
14. Uranium-235.
15. Acts 1:8.
16. 2 Corinthians 4:7.
17. John 1:36.
18. John 1:41-42.
19. Hebrews 11:1.
20. Slightly paraphrased from lyrics to a well-known hymn by Fanny Crosby: "Blessed Assurance," 1873.

CHAPTER 7: RUN TO THE BORDER

1. Rome Neal, "Official End of Legendary Feud," *CBS News*, June 13, 2003, https://www.cbsnews.com/news/official-end-of-legendary -feud/.
2. Scott Sauls, "Here's How God REALLY Sees You," *Scott Sauls* (blog), July 22, 2018, http://scottsauls.com/blog/2018/07/22/howgodseesyou/.
3. Scott Sauls, "Here's How God REALLY Sees You," *Scott Sauls* (blog), July 22, 2018.
4. Psalm 92:12-13.
5. Hugh Whelchel, "What Is Flourishing?" Institute for Faith, Work & Economics, May 20, 2013, https://tifwe.org/what-is-flourishing/.
6. Hugh Whelchel, "What Is Flourishing?" Institute for Faith, Work & Economics, May 20, 2013.
7. Jonathan T. Pennington, *The Sermon on the Mount and Human Flourishing: A Theological Commentary* (Grand Rapids, MI: Baker Academic, 2018), 47.
8. Pennington, *The Sermon on the Mount*, 149.
9. Matthew 5:9, KJV.
10. Leon Morris, *The Gospel according to Matthew*, Pillar New Testament Commentary (Grand Rapids, MI: Eerdmans, 1992), 101.
11. Eugene Peterson, *Eat This Book: A Conversation in the Art of Spiritual Reading* (Grand Rapids, MI: Eerdmans, 2009), 43–44. Quoted in Pennington, *The Sermon on the Mount*, 168.
12. God didn't sneak up on these people to bring judgment on them. Centuries had now passed since they'd first been warned, reaching back to the time of Abraham. Even during the conquest itself, people were given time to consider and avoid what was coming. There were those who thankfully and willingly ran from such practices toward God, and,

as Gleason Archer suggests, most women and children would've fled before actual battles, so no one knows how this worked among those not fighting. For information on Canaanite religious practices, see Paul Copan, *Is God a Moral Monster: Making Sense of the Old Testament God* (Grand Rapids, MI: BakerBooks, 2011), 159–61.

13. Genesis 18:25.
14. Joshua 22:1-5, author's paraphrase.
15. Joshua 22:10.
16. Joshua 22:11-12.
17. See Numbers 25.
18. Joshua 22:16.
19. Joshua 22:18.
20. Ephesians 4:15.
21. Joshua 22:19, author's paraphrase.
22. Joshua 22:22, author's paraphrase.
23. Joshua 22:27, author's paraphrase.
24. Joshua 24-27, author's paraphrase.
25. Joshua 22:32.
26. Joshua 22:33.
27. Joshua 22:34.

CHAPTER 8: ANTIFRAGILE . . . SORT OF

1. Front Page Africa, "Liberia: ODF Communities in Margibi Didn't Experience Ebola Virus," AllAfrica.com, March 25, 2015, https://allafrica.com/stories/201503250829.html.
2. John Newton, "Amazing Grace," 1772.
3. *Online Etymology Dictionary*, s.v. "resilient (adj.)," accessed February 28, 2020, https://www.etymonline.com/word/resilient.
4. *Merriam-Webster*, s.v. "resilience, *n.*," accessed January 23, 2020, https://www.merriam-webster.com/dictionary/resilience.
5. Nassim Nicholas Taleb, *Antifragile: Things that Gain from Disorder* (New York: Random House, 2014), 3.
6. Taleb, *Antifragile*, 3.
7. Taleb, *Antifragile*, 42.
8. Alas, I do not think Mr. Taleb will be too worried about such an observation from me. (He's too antifragile for that.)
9. James 1:2-4.
10. Romans 5:3-5, NASB.
11. 2 Corinthians 12:10.
12. 2 Corinthians 4:7, ESV.
13. Quoted in Hugh Whelchel, "Four Defining Characteristics of Biblical

Flourishing," Institute for Faith, Work and Economics, June 12, 2014, https://tifwe.org/four-defining-characteristics-biblical-flourishing/.

14. Peter wrote this in Rome even though he says in the letter he's writing from "Babylon." See https://bible.org/article/introduction-book-1-peter.

15. *Corrects Jesus*: Matthew 26:33-35; John 13:6-9; Acts 10:14-19; *skip the cross*: Matthew 16:22-23.

16. 1 Peter 5:6.

17. Proverbs 3:34.

18. James 4:6.

19. 1 Peter 5:5.

20. Exodus 3:19.

21. Deuteronomy 3:24.

22. Walter Bauer, *A Greek-English Lexicon of the New Testament and Other Early Christian Literature*, revised and edited by Frederick William Danker (Chicago: University of Chicago Press, 1979), 990.

23. Brené Brown, *Dare to Lead: Brave Work, Tough Conversations, Whole Hearts* (New York: Random House, 2018), part one, section one.

24. Brown, *Dare to Lead*, 24.

25. 1 Peter 5:7, ESV.

26. Rebekah Lyons, *Rhythms of Renewal: Trading Stress and Anxiety for a Life of Peace and Purpose* (Grand Rapids, MI: Zondervan, 2019), 287.

27. Lauren F. Winner, *Still: Notes on a Mid-Faith Crisis* (New York: HarperOne, 2012), 89.

28. See, for example, John Ortberg, "Joyful Confidence in God: the Dark Night of the Soul," Faith Gateway, September 26, 2017, https://www.faithgateway.com/joyful-confidence-god-dark-night-soul/#.XlkxIahKjIV.

29. 1 Peter 5:6.

30. 1 Peter 5:10.

31. Dan Allender, *To Be Told: God Invites You to Coauthor Your Future* (Colorado Springs: Waterbrook, 2006), 47.

CHAPTER 9: ZAMBEZI OVERLOAD

1. Batoka Gorge.

2. "The Batoka Rapids, Zambezi River," Zambezi.com, accessed February 28, 2020, https://www.zambezi.com/blog/2012/the-batoka-rapids-zambezi-river/.

3. John Ortberg, *If You Want to Walk on Water, You've Got to Get Out of the Boat* (Grand Rapids, MI: Zondervan, 2014), 176–77.

4. Ortberg, *If You Want to Walk on Water*, 176–77.

5. Daniel Goleman, *Emotional Intelligence: Why It Can Matter More than IQ* (New York: Bantam, 2005), 177.

6. Proverbs 13:12.
7. Ortberg, *If You Want to Walk on Water*, 180.
8. Goleman, *Emotional Intelligence*, 87.
9. Alex Korb, *The Upward Spiral: Using Neuroscience to Reverse the Course of Depression, One Small Change at a Time* (Oakland, CA: New Harbinger, 2015), 106.
10. Jeremy Weber, "80% of Churchgoers Don't Read Bible Daily, Lifeway Survey Says," *Christianity Today*, September 7, 2012, https://www .christianitytoday.com/news/2012/september/80-of-churchgoers -dont-read-bible-daily-lifeway-survey.html.
11. Korb, *The Upward Spiral*, 124.
12. See the plaque at the John F. Kennedy Presidential Library and Museum, https://www.jfklibrary.org/asset-viewer/breton-fishermans -prayer-plaque.
13. Jeremiah 15:15, 18, Voice.
14. Korb, *The Upward Spiral*, 44.
15. Romans 8:26.
16. Poem entitled "For the Family and Friends of a Suicide," from John O'Donohue, *To Bless the Space Between Us: A Book of Blessings* (New York: Doubleday, 2008), 162.
17. Jeremiah 16:19, Voice.
18. Korb, *The Upward Spiral*, 151.
19. Psalm 139:13-14.
20. Johnson Oatman Jr., "Count Your Blessings," 1897, https://library .timelesstruths.org/music/Count_Your_Blessings/.
21. Korb, *The Upward Spiral*, 160.
22. Exodus 6:6.
23. The Hebrew verb *natsal* implies an abrupt physical act of grasping or seizing. For more information see Walter Brueggemann, *Theology of the Old Testament: Testimony, Dispute, Advocacy* (Minneapolis: Fortress Press, 1997), 174.

CHAPTER 10: MUPPETS IN THE BALCONY

1. *Marvel Team-Up* 74, October 1978, https://muppet.fandom.com/wiki /Marvel_Comics?file=Marvel_Team-Up_74.jpg.
2. Proverbs 18:2.
3. Dave D'Alessio and Mike Allen, "The Selective Exposure Hypothesis and Media Choice Processes," in *Mass Media Effects Research: Advances through Meta-Analysis*, ed. Raymond W. Preiss et al. (Mahwah, NJ: Erlbaum, 2007), 103–19.
4. C Thi Nguyen, "Escape the Echo Chamber," *Aeon Magazine*, April 9,

2018, https://aeon.co/essays/why-its-as-hard-to-escape-an-echo
-chamber-as-it-is-to-flee-a-cult.

5. See Eli Pariser, *The Filter Bubble: How the New Personalized Web Is
    Changing What We Read and How We Think* (New York: Penguin, 2011)
    and Cass Sunstein, *#Republic: Divided Democracy in the Age of Social
    Media* (Princeton, NJ: Princeton University Press, 2017).

6. C Thi Nguyen, "Escape the Echo Chamber," *Aeon Magazine*, April 9,
    2018.

7. John R. W. Stott, *The Message of the Sermon on the Mount: Christian
    Counter-Culture* (Downers Grove, IL: InterVarsity Press, 1992), 65,
    quoted in Michael Wear, *Reclaiming Hope: Lessons Learned in the Obama
    White House about the Future of Faith in America* (Nashville: Nelson
    Books, 2017), 211.

8. DOMO, "Data Never Sleeps 5.0," accessed January 23, 2020, https://
    www.domo.com/learn/data-never-sleeps-5.

9. Greg Holder, *The Genius of One: God's Answer for Our Fractured World*
    (Colorado Springs: NavPress, 2017), 161.

10. "Slacktivism," Techopedia.com, accessed January 23, 2020, https://
    www.techopedia.com/definition/28252/slacktivism. Emphasis mine.

11. David Anderson, *Gracism: The Art of Inclusion* (Downers Grove, IL:
    IVP Books, 2007), 158–59.

12. Esther 3:13.

13. Esther 4:14. Emphasis mine.

14. Jeremiah 38:9, VOICE.

15. John 15:18-19.

16. Ephesians 6:19-20.

17. Theodore Roosevelt, "Citizenship in a Republic," speech at the Sorbonne,
    Paris, April 23, 1910, *The Works of Theodore Roosevelt*, vol. 13 (New York:
    Charles Scribner's Sons, 1926), 506–29.

18. Theodore Roosevelt, "Citizenship in a Republic," Speech at the Sorbonne,
    Paris, April 23, 1910.

19. Ephesians 2:10.

20. To reference this passage in the New Jerusalem Bible, see https://
    www.bibliacatolica.com.br/en/new-jerusalem-bible/ephesians/2/.

21. Anthony Bradley, "The New Legalism: Missional, Radical, Narcissistic,
    and Shamed," Acton Institute Powerblog, May 1, 2013, https://
    blog.acton.org/archives/53944-the-new-legalism-missional-radical
    -narcissistic-and-shamed.html.

22. 1 Corinthians 10:31.

23. 1 Corinthians 15:58.

24. Abraham Kuyper, "Sphere Sovereignty," in *Abraham Kuyper, A Centennial
    Reader*, ed. James D. Bratt (Grand Rapids, MI: Eerdmans, 1998), 488.

CHAPTER 11: WELCOME ABOARD

1. *Proslambanō*; see https://www.blueletterbible.org/lang/lexicon/lexicon
.cfm?Strongs=G4355&t=NIV.
2. Greg Holder, *The Genius of One: God's Answer for Our Fractured World*
(Colorado Springs: NavPress, 2017), ix.
3. Daniel Goleman, *Emotional Intelligence: Why It Can Matter More than
IQ* (New York: Bantam, 2005), 37, citing a study by James House et al.,
"Social Relationships and Health," *Science*, July 29, 1988.
4. Jeremiah 29:5-7, Voice.
5. Soong-Chan Rah, "Freeing the Captive Church," *Faith & Leadership*,
September 12, 2011, https://faithandleadership.com/soong-chan-rah
-freeing-captive-church. Emphasis added.
6. Christine D. Pohl, *Making Room: Recovering Hospitality as a Christian
Tradition* (Grand Rapids, MI: Eerdmans, 1999), 72.
7. Genesis 18:2.
8. Genesis 18:4-5, author's paraphrase.
9. Derek Kidner, *Genesis*, Tyndale Old Testament Commentaries
(Downers Grove, IL: InterVarsity Press, 2008), 142.
10. Henri Nouwen, *Reaching Out: the Three Movements of the Spiritual Life*
(Broadway, NY: Image Books, 1986), 66.
11. Miyoung Yoon Hammer, "Restoring Hospitality: A Blessing for
Visitor and Host—A Conversation with Christine Pohl," Fuller Studio,
accessed January 23, 2020, https://fullerstudio.fuller.edu/restoring
-hospitality-blessing-visitor-host/.
12. Luke 19:5-10.
13. Revelation 3:20.
14. Hebrews 13:1-2.
15. Christopher J. H. Wright, *The God I Don't Understand: Reflections
on Tough Questions of Faith* (Grand Rapids, MI: Zondervan, 2008),
107.
16. Wright, *The God I Don't Understand*, 107.
17. Romans 12:13.
18. Philippians 3:14.
19. Nouwen, *Reaching Out*, 71.
20. See Genesis 3:24.
21. Thank you to Robert Gallagher, OA, for his conceptualization of this
in "The Three Movements of the Spiritual Life: Part Two—From
Hostility to Hospitality," Congregational Development, January 22,
2013, http://www.congregationaldevelopment.com/means-of-grace
-hope-of-glory/2013/1/22/the-three-movements-of-the-spiritual-life
-part-two-from-host.html.
22. Nouwen, *Reaching Out*, 19.

23. Nouwen, *Reaching Out*, 98.
24. 1 Peter 4:9.
25. Lorne Sanny, quoted in Mark Buchanan, *Your God Is Too Safe: Rediscovering the Wonder of a God You Can't Control* (Colorado Springs: Multnomah Books, 2001), 212.
26. Ann Voskamp, "After Charlottesville, the Question We Absolutely Have to Answer: Who Is Willing to Pick Up Their Cross?" August 14, 2017, https://annvoskamp.com/2017/08/after-charlottesville-the -question-we-absolutely-have-to-answer-who-is-willing-to-pick-up -their-cross/.
27. Proverbs 29:20.
28. Hebrews 13:2.
29. C. S. Lewis, *The Weight of Glory* (San Francisco: HarperOne, 2001), 46.
30. John Calvin, *Institutes of the Christian Religion*, ed. John T. McNeill (Philadelphia: Westminster Press, 1960), 696.
31. Calvin, *Institutes*, 696.
32. 1 Corinthians 13:12.
33. Margaret Feinberg, *Taste and See: Discovering God Among Butchers, Bakers, and Fresh Food Makers* (Grand Rapids, MI: Zondervan, 2019), 15.

EPILOGUE: MUSIC OF THE DAWN

1. Seth S. Horowitz, *The Universal Sense: How Hearing Shapes the Mind* (New York: Bloomsbury, 2012), 113.
2. Seth Horowitz, "Sound a Major Emotional Driver for Humans," *All Things Considered*, September 7, 2012, https://www.npr.org/2012/09 /07/160766898/sound-a-major-emotional-driver-for-humans.
3. Horowitz, "Sound a Major Emotional Driver for Humans."
4. Julian Treasure, "How Can We All Listen Better?" interview by Guy Raz, TED Radio Hour, NPR, March 7, 2014.
5. Psalm 1:1, ESV.
6. Colossians 2:8.
7. Romans 8:22.
8. N. T. Wright, *Simply Christian: Why Christianity Makes Sense* (San Francisco: HarperOne, 2010), 237.
9. See https://www.nytimes.com/2012/11/11/opinion/sunday/why -listening-is-so-much-more-than-hearing.html.
10. Michael Horton, *Rediscovering the Holy Spirit: God's Perfecting Presence in Creation, Redemption, and Everyday Life* (Grand Rapids, MI: Zondervan, 2017) 24.
11. Romans 8:16.
12. 1 Corinthians 3:16, ESV.
13. John 14:17.

BE THE ANSWER TO PRAYER

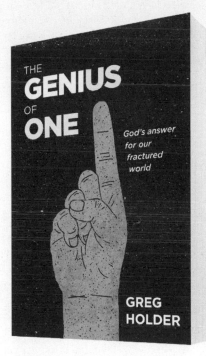

THE
GENIUS
OF
ONE

*God's answer
for our
fractured
world*

**GREG
HOLDER**

The world is fractured. Tensions are high, patience is low, and goodwill is hard to come by. Tracing back to a prayer Jesus prayed on the worst night of his life, "That they"—that we—"would be one," author and pastor Greg Holder takes his readers on a winding journey from that glorious prayer to the practical realities of their everyday lives. For those who cling to the hope that God is still at work, this book will both stir a deeper longing for a better way and provide practical steps toward that way.

CP1617

THE NAVIGATORS® STORY

———————— ◗ ————————

T HANK YOU for picking up this NavPress book! I hope it has been a blessing to you.

NavPress is a ministry of The Navigators. The Navigators began in the 1930s, when a young California lumberyard worker named Dawson Trotman was impacted by basic discipleship principles and felt called to teach those principles to others. He saw this mission as an echo of 2 Timothy 2:2: "And the things you have heard me say in the presence of many witnesses entrust to reliable people who will also be qualified to teach others" (NIV).

In 1933, Trotman and his friends began discipling members of the US Navy. By the end of World War II, thousands of men on ships and bases around the world were learning the principles of spiritual multiplication by the intentional, person-to-person teaching of God's Word.

After World War II, The Navigators expanded its relational ministry to include college campuses; local churches; the Glen Eyrie Conference Center and Eagle Lake Camps in Colorado Springs, Colorado; and neighborhood and citywide initiatives across the country and around the world.

Today, with more than 2,600 US staff members—and local ministries in more than 100 countries—The Navigators continues the transformational process of making disciples who make more disciples, advancing the Kingdom of God in a world that desperately needs the hope and salvation of Jesus Christ and the encouragement to grow deeper in relationship with Him.

NavPress was created in 1975 to advance the calling of The Navigators by bringing biblically rooted and culturally relevant products to people who want to know and love Christ more deeply. In January 2014, NavPress entered an alliance with Tyndale House Publishers to strengthen and better position our rich content for the future. Through *THE MESSAGE* Bible and other resources, NavPress seeks to bring positive spiritual movement to people's lives.

If you're interested in learning more or becoming involved with The Navigators, go to www.navigators.org. For more discipleship content from The Navigators and NavPress authors, visit www.thedisciplemaker.org. May God bless you in your walk with Him!

Sincerely,

DON PAPE
VP/PUBLISHER, NAVPRESS

www.navpress.com

CP1308